AF240888

SOCCER CLUB GEOPOLITICS

Kévin Veyssière

Soccer club geopolitics
22 unusual stories to understand the world

Max Milo, Paris, 2023
www.maxmilo.com
ISBN : 978-2-315-01129-2

PREFACE

Kévin Veyssière created a page on social networks, "FC Geopolitics", which quickly became very successful and attracted the attention of a growing audience. The reasons for this success are very simple: combining the seriousness of a documentation work with a judicious choice of illustrations. The subjects he tackles arouse curiosity, but they are far from being anecdotal: they lead to in-depth reflection, all in a pleasant tone. Kévin Veyssière likes to surprise us and take us on roundabout ways. He manages to show that soccer is a very serious subject and that geopolitics can be pleasant. The small stories are at the rendezvous of the big one and he takes us there in an attractive way.

Kévin Veyssière reminds us of the time when Franco's Spain refused to play against the USSR, or the way Croatia used its national team to obtain international recognition. Closer to home, he evokes the "impossible matches" of the Kosovo team, those between Gibraltar and Spain or Armenia and Azerbaijan. It can go from what may seem anecdotal *at first* (Tuvalu) to the heaviest (the Qatar-Saudi Arabia duel). It is always precise and pleasant.

In the early days of European soccer competitions, before the advent of mass television and social networks, many teenagers learned about European geography by reading the results of foreign championships and European cups. No doubt, in a few years, many people will say that they became interested in geopolitics through Kévin Veyssière's stories, seeking to broaden their knowledge after realizing that no, geopolitics is not boring and uninteresting, and that it is not reserved for seasoned diplomats and staff officers.

Shortly before the 1998 World Cup, I had proposed to two publishers, one academic, the other general public, to write a book on the theme of soccer and international relations. Both of them did not laugh in my face, out of politeness. They didn't think less of me. With courtesy, they made me understand that, since I had a passion for something like soccer, which was a trifle, I could eventually do a book on this subject. But they were pushing me to do a book on international relations instead, since that was my profession and my specialty. They saw absolutely no connection between the two, and they advised me against pursuing this pipe dream.

Soccer is now less despised by the intellectual elites, and geopolitics is widely rehabilitated. Associating soccer and geopolitics is now obvious. Kévin Veyssière illustrates this with talent. He succeeds in opening the curiosity of soccer fans to geopolitics and demonstrates, to those interested in geostrategic issues, that soccer can be part of it.

Pascal Boniface

Introduction

In June 2021 will be held the 16th edition of the Euro, the major international event of European soccer. Still soccer you say? However, this competition has more than just a sporting interest, since its creation in 1960, the Euro has not ceased to break down barriers and to ease relations between European nations, already shaken at the time by the two world wars. It is no coincidence that the Union of European Football Associations (UEFA), which created this summer tournament, was born at the same time as the political and economic construction of Europe, with the signing of the Treaties of Rome in 1957. The idea was to reunite the European continent through sport and to find a new terrain, other than the battlefield, on which nations could compete.

The bet seems to be successful since today the UEFA organization gathers nearly 55 member countries, which is much more than the European Union (27) or the Council of Europe (47). Football has succeeded in crossing borders, even beyond the continent. The Europe of soccer now extends to Kazakhstan! Today, soccer embraces all strata of society and acts as a revelation of the strengths and weaknesses of each state on our planet.

On the sporting field, the matches replace the old warlike confrontations, as it can be the case when England and Scotland face each other. Or they allow nations to reveal themselves, as in the case of Croatia at Euro 1996, which was able to wear its checkered shirt, a national symbol, for the first time in an international soccer competition. A situation that will be experienced by North Macedonia as its team participates for the first time in the Euro this summer. An opportunity to bring the little-known history of this young country, with a new name since 2018, to millions of viewers.

The world's most popular sport is a formidable showcase, synonymous for states with leverage to attract their territory: a *soft power* tool[1], to shine and seduce in the eyes of the world; a source of influence that can be used to bring a country out of anonymity or change its image. This is the path taken by Qatar, which has become a key player in the world of football, culminating in the future organization of the 2022 World Cup. The emirate›s desire to shine too brightly may well burn its wings. The recent revelations in the *Guardian* newspaper[2] about the number of dead workers on the World Cup construction sites will indeed weaken the Qatari country. Proof that diplomacy through sport can have its limits and that it can ultimately do more harm than good.

Moreover, national teams have such an ambassadorial role that a soccer match can be like a new battle. Like when the Hong Kong team's victory over China triggered riots in Beijing in 1985. Or when the famous Argentine player Diego Maradona "avenged" the Falklands War by defeating England in the 1986 World Cup.

---

1. "Soft power is that soft power, which has become the new and subtle form of power, where each state tries to attract the attention, respect and sympathy of other nations," BONIFACE Pascal, *Geopolitics of Sport*, Armand Colin, 2014.
2. MCINTYRE Niamh, PATTISSON Pete, "Revealed: 6,500 migrant workers have died in Qatar since World Cup awarded," *The Guardian*, February 2021.

The situation is sometimes such that, in some cases, matches are impossible. Kosovo, whose state existence is not internationally recognized, is in this situation. Its national team simply cannot play against certain other countries. When the real war gets involved, soccer has no place as an instrument of peace, as is the case between Armenia and Azerbaijan in the Nagorno-Karabakh region.

Beyond the simple meetings between respective countries, soccer can also be the source of beautiful stories to promote the autonomy of a country. Like the epic of the "Eleven of Independence" in the 1960s, in its quest for a free Algeria. Practices that are reproduced today through the example of Greenland, a gigantic Danish territory that is seeking a path to independence through football. Thousands of kilometers away from the Arctic, Easter Island also uses soccer to work towards the recognition of the Rapa Nui culture; proof that this sport can allow populations and regions to reach greater autonomy. Finally, soccer can be a great alert on the urgent issue of global warming, and thus save what can be left of the Tuvalu Islands in Oceania.

Far from being exhaustive, this book invites the curious, soccer fans or budding geographers, to travel the world through soccer stories and great sporting moments, while helping to understand the political, economic and social issues of our planet.

Soccer is not just about the ball.

Kévin VEYSSIÈRE

Part 1:

EUROPE

I. The Euro soccer tournament, a history intimately linked to that of Europe

1.

THE EURO SOCCER TOURNAMENT IN THE FOOTSTEPS OF EUROPEAN CONSTRUCTION

The European Football Championship was born at the same time as the beginnings of the European economic and political construction. This is not a coincidence, as the decision-makers of the different countries of the continent were trying at the time to unite, and thus not to repeat the mistakes of the previous world wars. In a certain way, the Euro soccer tournament will have allowed to push back the borders. The football will pierce the "iron curtain" and will allow the nations of the Western and Eastern blocks to meet on another ground than that of the cold war.

Europe is the birthplace of soccer. The first real club was founded in England in 1857, in the city of Sheffield. The first international soccer match in history was played in England on November 30, 1872 against Scotland. The game was then exported throughout the continent and the world, thanks to the traders, settlers and representatives of the British Empire. It was so successful that other teams were created. The first match between two non-British national teams took place in Vienna between Austria and Hungary on

1. The Euro soccer tournament in the footsteps of European construction

October 12, 1902. Faced with the internationalization of the *English Game*, the teams from across the Channel gradually began to close in on themselves, presenting themselves as the great patrons of their sport. It must be said that the English team collected successes in its first away games, including a severe 15-0 victory over France in 1906. In other European countries, many clubs emerged and organized themselves to counter the British hegemony, which was both sporting and political at the time.

Sport, as an instrument to ease international tensions, has moreover the wind in its sails since the first modern Olympic Games were created in 1896, at the initiative of the Frenchman Pierre de Coubertin. Soccer follows the same path. On May 21, 1904, the Fédération Internationale de Football Association, more commonly known today as FIFA, was founded in Paris. The founding members were European: Belgium, Denmark, Spain, France, the Netherlands, Sweden and Switzerland. The international matches were limited to friendly matches. The reference tournament of the time was the Olympic Games, where the British team won the 1908 and 1912 editions. The First World War, from 1914 to 1918, shook Europe, reshuffling the cards of the powers that be. Not to mention the human disaster that resulted from this terrible conflict, with more than 20 million victims.

Sport could have been one of the levers for the construction of a peaceful Europe at the end of the war, but the Versailles peace treaty, signed in 1919, clearly shows that the victorious nations sought above all to weaken the competing powers even more, rather than to seek a possible compromise. This discrepancy does not help the construction of a political Europe. At the same time, new actors are competing with the European nations at their own game. This is already the case at the level of omnisports, since the United

States settled from 1920 on top of the table of medals of the various editions of the Olympic Games. At the level of the round ball, new nations are also invited. The tournament of soccer of the Olympic Games is always the only true international competition of soccer. In 1920, Egypt was the first non-Western team to compete in this competition, soon joined by Uruguay in 1924. It is besides this last country which wins the tournament this year against Switzerland. The situation is worse for Europe in 1928, since no European team is in the final! Uruguay won again at the expense of Argentina.

The British nations and Europe no longer have a monopoly on soccer. Above all, FIFA is beginning to think seriously about creating a large-scale international tournament, as the last two finals of the Olympic tournament were attended by more than 30,000 spectators. FIFA is allowing professional players to participate in this development, as many European countries have already started to create their own leagues. This does not please the International Olympic Committee (IOC), which wants to preserve the value of amateurism at its Games. This disagreement will lead to the creation of the first World Cup of soccer, in 1930.

The choice of the organizer is the team in vogue at the moment, Uruguay. Officially to celebrate the country's centenary, unofficially because Uruguay agreed to pay the participation fees of the teams and to build a new stadium dedicated to the final of this new world competition. Although the Uruguayan team won the first edition, the following editions were held in Europe, in 1934 in Italy and in 1938 in France. The soccer craze in those years was not used to bring nations together. As shown by the organization of the 1934 World Cup in Mussolini's Italy, or the 1936 Olympic Games in Nazi Germany, sport was used to legitimize the dictatorial regimes of the host countries.

1. The Euro soccer tournament in the footsteps of European construction

However, the idea of creating a European competition is well present since, as early as 1927, Henri Delaunay, secretary general of the French Football Federation, pushes for the organization of an international tournament on the European continent. The creation of the World Cup sounded the death knell for this project. It was not until the end of the Second World War that the idea resurfaced, this time with the firm intention of bringing people together through sport and not making the same mistakes as in the past. At the end of the war, while the "fathers" of Europe (Jean Monnet, Robert Schuman, Paul-Henri Spaak) were working on the economic and political construction of Europe, three other men were going to elaborate the sports union of the continent: the Italian Ottorino Barassi, the Belgian José Crahay and the French Henri Delaunay. Things have been moving since 1953, when FIFA lifted the ban on the creation of continental federations. This decision was taken following pressure from European countries in the face of the growing influence of South American nations. The first post-war World Cup, in 1950, ended with Uruguay's victory over Brazil. Moreover, soccer was becoming more international and the weight of the Europeans on the decisions of FIFA was beginning to melt.

These two trends, namely to counter the leadership of South America in soccer as well as to strengthen the logic of bringing people together - with the creation of the Council of Europe in 1949 and the European Coal and Steel Community (ECSC) in 1952 - gave rise to the idea of creating a European soccer organization. On June 15, 1954, the Union of European Football Associations (UEFA) was founded in the Swiss city of Basel - a federation that went beyond mere politics, with 25 delegates representing 30 soccer associations, including those from the Eastern Bloc. Since the end of the

Second World War, Europe has been divided in two by an "iron curtain". This expression symbolizes the political border dividing the European continent into two distinct zones: a Western bloc composed of European states turned towards the United States and an Eastern bloc composed of European states under the influence of the USSR. Soccer is one of the few ways in which this political boundary can be blurred somewhat.

The creation of UEFA should logically have led to the creation of a European competition between the different national teams. While the Copa America in South America has existed since 1916, the project of a European equivalent has been slow to materialize. The death in 1954 of Henri Delaunay, one of the founders of UEFA, was another obstacle. Meanwhile, the clubs were getting organized. Following an article in the *Daily Mirror* in December 1954, which proclaimed that the English club Wolverhampton deserved the title of European champion after two victories against Budapest Honvéd and Spartak Moscow, the French newspaper *L'Équipe* counterattacked. It proposes, on the initiative of its journalist Gabriel Hanot, the creation of a European cup to prove that the British hegemony on the football is far from being acquired[3]. This idea is in line with another one, as the sports daily has been looking for a few years to create a competition to improve the sales of its newspapers in the middle of the week.

On April 3, 1955, the newspaper *L'Équipe* and the presidents of the main European clubs decided to create the European Champion Clubs' Cup, which is neither more nor less than the ancestor of the Champions League as we know it today. The first edition of this European Cup was launched during the 1955-1956 season. If UEFA

3. MOUTON Olivier, *Hors-Jeu. 22 soccer matches that made history*, Armand Colin, 2017 - chap. 6, p. 61.

did not intervene immediately in this matter, it is above all because Henri Delaunay was no longer in charge and that the organization had been created at the beginning with a political aim, namely to defend the European positions within FIFA, rather than to set up sporting competitions.

This European Cup was so popular (with nearly 124,000 spectators in the Santiago-Bernabéu stadium for the 1957 final between Real Madrid and Fiorentina) that the idea of creating a competition between the main national teams resurfaced within the UEFA authorities. After much wrangling with FIFA, the principle of a European championship of nations, or Euro soccer, was agreed in June 1958 in Stockholm. One year earlier, the Treaties of Rome were signed, laying the foundations of a European Economic Community (EEC).

There was still the hazardous task of convincing the national federations to take part in this future Euro, which was to take place between 1958 and 1960. Pierre Delaunay, Henri's son, embarked on a tour to convince 17 national federations to participate in this first competition. As with the European Club Cup, this sports tournament brought together countries beyond the "Iron Curtain", as even the USSR agreed. The very first match of this championship took place on September 28, 1958: the USSR met Hungary in the Central Lenin Stadium in Moscow, where more than 100,000 people came to watch the match. Other matches allowed nations from different blocs to meet. Like on April 5, 1959, when the Republic of Ireland, a western nation, met Czechoslovakia, an eastern nation.

Over the years, the Euro continues to grow and break down borders. For the 2021 edition, 55 UEFA member national teams are participating in the qualifiers. 24 teams will compete in the final phase this summer. This makes the "Europe of soccer" an important lever for the construction of Europe as a continent, and even beyond, since national soccer teams such as those of Israel or Kazakhstan are well present. The European Football Championship has thus achieved its main objective, that of widening the European borders and pushing back, hopefully for a long time, the spectre of war.

2.
Euro 1960: when Franco's Spain refused to play against the USSR

The first Euro soccer tournament, in 1960, was a real boon for UEFA, which had the ambition to make its tournament the most watched competition on the planet. However, a decisive match between the two main favorites, Spain and the USSR, turned this sporting moment into a political moment. It highlights the major differences that still oppose Europe, the ideological division between the Western and Eastern blocks and the Cold War.

We left Euro 1960, in the previous chapter, with one of the games that went beyond the European divisions of the Cold War, the one between the Republic of Ireland and Czechoslovakia. In this game, it was the Eastern team that qualified for the rest of this European Championship of Nations. A competition that sees 17 selections compete, but some major European teams, such as England, Germany and Italy, have declined the invitation. The reason: they have doubts about the success of this new tournament. However, France, third of the 1958 World Cup, Sweden, finalist of this World Cup against Brazil, and Spain, with many players from Real Madrid, are there.

The Madrid club is installed on the roof of Europe since its team has won all the titles of the European Champion Clubs' Cup since 1956 and gathers the best players of the moment, in particular Alfredo Di Stéfano. So, Spain is the scarecrow for this first Euro. To reach the final phase of the competition, the teams involved must play two more rounds in round robin matches, a sort of round of 16 and quarter-finals before their time. The main favourites have no trouble distinguishing themselves during their warm-up round. The UEFA, organizer of the competition, can keep smiling.

A shadow slips into the picture in the next round. The USSR team, which has easily disposed of Hungary, meets in the quarterfinals Spain. An attractive match on paper, between the two footballing forces of the moment. The Soviets have, in fact, won the soccer event at the 1956 Olympic Games in Melbourne. However, the meeting will never take place. Because of one man: Franco. The military dictator had been in power in Spain since 1939. To achieve this, he had to win the Spanish Civil War between 1936 and 1939, during which the USSR supported the People's Army of the Spanish Republic, while fascist Italy and Nazi Germany supported Franco's nationalist regime.

The "Caudillo", Franco's nickname, keeps this "betrayal" in mind. Nine days before the first leg, a council of ministers was held to decide whether the Spanish team should play the Soviet team in the Euro 1960. Four days later, the decision was made. It is decided that the Spanish team will not face the USSR. A decision justified in the texts by the fact that Spanish soldiers of the Azul division, put at the disposal by Spain of the Wehrmacht during the Second World

War to fight on the Russian front, would be still retained prisoners in the gulags of Siberia.

Just before leaving for the game, the Spanish team was left grounded. Legend has it that the Spanish star, Di Stéfano, lamented, "Why? Why?" he said to a federation official. "Why? Franco's order"[4], he was told. It must be said that the military general did not like the fact that the Spanish team could suffer a defeat in Moscow and thus deal a direct blow to the legitimacy and effectiveness of his political regime. The old demons of the Spanish Civil War could also have resurfaced if "Soviet ambassadors" in spikes had come to the capital Madrid.

In any case, this decision is terrible for UEFA, which does not want the political decisions of member countries to interfere with the smooth running of its competition, presented as apolitical. The newspapers, for their part, were quick to draw their conclusions. Agence France-Presse headlined at the time: "Football is a victim of the Cold War".[5] UEFA then tried everything and proposed a compromise. The match would be played on a neutral ground. If the Spanish regime accepted, the Soviets on the other hand refused this decision. Destitute, the authority of the European soccer can only abdicate and announce the qualification of the USSR. Spain, excluded, receives a fine of 2,000 Swiss francs. The great Spanish generation of the time, which dominated European soccer with Real Madrid, lost the opportunity to win a major international title. Especially Di Stéfano, who will not win any title with Spain.

On the Soviet side, the team has the privilege to participate in the first Euro soccer finals in history. For this part of the competition

---

4. MOUTON Olivier, *Hors-Jeu. 22 matchs de soccer qui ont marqué l'histoire,* Armand Colin, 2017 - chap. 8, p. 83.
5. MOUTON Olivier, *Hors-Jeu. 22 soccer matches that made history,* Armand Colin, 2017 - chap. 8, p. 84.

between the last four qualified teams, the matches are no longer played in a round robin format, but in a knockout match. UEFA chose France to host the final round, in honor of Henri Delaunay. This does not bring luck to Les Bleus, since they lose in the semi-final against Yugoslavia, while the USSR defeats Czechoslovakia.

The final, on July 10, 1960 at the Parc des Princes stadium in Paris, had all the makings of a political meeting. Now leader of the non-aligned movement, Yugoslavia, governed by General Tito, has indeed cut its relations with the USSR since 1948. A Yugoslav victory would be seen as a triumph on the Soviet model. Especially since the players were promised a piece of land in case of victory. However, in the final match, the legendary Soviet goalkeeper Lev Yashin tamed the Balkan offensives, and it was the striker Viktor Ponedelnik who propelled the "Red Army" to the top of European soccer. A victory that brings relief.

The USSR has already crossed the road of Yugoslavia during the Olympic soccer tournament in 1952, in Helsinki. The Yugoslav victory led to a black anger of Stalin, who severely punished the players of the team and the coach of the time. In 1960, the honor is now restored. The Soviet regime can boast, with this sporting victory, that its political model prevails over others, especially those of the West. Especially since the final podium of this first Euro consecrates three national teams of Eastern Europe, with the USSR, Yugoslavia and Czechoslovakia.

Is Franco biting his fingers? History does not tell us. Meanwhile, the Spanish players are mostly consoled with a new European title of Real Madrid, with a victory 7 goals to 3, against Eintracht Frankfurt. Proof that Spain is in good shape, the 1960 Ballon d'Or is awarded to the FC Barcelona player Luis Suarez. The golden generation did not lose everything, however. Franco had his revenge four years later, at the second edition of the Euro in 1964.

This time, Spain qualified for the finals, and even offered to organize it. A great opportunity to put the person of Franco and his political regime in the foreground. UEFA imposed a condition that the tournament should be played in Spain. The team of the USSR, also qualified, must be able to participate. The European leaders want to avoid a new crisis, especially since the competition has grown, with 27 teams that participated in the qualifiers.

The finals were held in Spain and the host country faced Denmark, Hungary and, of course, the USSR. While the Soviets easily qualified for the final, Spain almost missed this appointment because it needed a final goal in extra time to get rid of the Hungarian team. The long-awaited match took place on June 21, 1964.

In front of nearly 80,000 people in the boiling Santiago Bernabeu stadium in Madrid, and especially in front of Franco himself, La Roja's players simply can't afford to make any mistakes. The game started with a bang. Barcelona's Jesús Perada opened the scoring in the sixth minute. Two minutes later, Spartak Moscow striker Galimzian Khusaynov answered. Lev Yashin, once again, kept the opponents at bay, but it was the Spaniard Marcelino who finally allowed this great Spanish team to win its first international title.

A consecration for Spanish soccer, but also for Franco, who was looking for another great sporting victory, in addition to that of Real Madrid in the European Cup, to shine a little more in the international landscape. The 1964 European Championship was the only achievement of the Spanish team under Franco's regime. It was not until the 1990s, and especially the historic treble Euro-Cup-Euro from 2008 to 2012, to see the Spanish soccer shine again.

3.

When geopolitics reshuffles the cards at Euro 1992

In 1992, the Euro should crown one of the main favorites, English, German, French or Dutch. However, the soccer tournament was turned upside down by the fall of the USSR and the Balkan wars. A surprise guest caused a sensation: Denmark, which took advantage of the exclusion of Yugoslavia in the middle of a conflict to reveal itself to the eyes of the continent and write one of the most beautiful pages in the history of European soccer.

The Euro 1992 is a double event: on the one hand, it is the first European championship of soccer nations after the fall of the USSR and, on the other hand, it thwarts all predictions, with Denmark as the unexpected winner. This victory would not have been possible without the many geopolitical upheavals of this period. Indeed, the beginning of the 1990s opened a new era for Europe. The fall of the Berlin Wall on November 9, 1989, symbolized the end of the political frontier of the "Iron Curtain" in Europe, which led to the fall of the various communist regimes in the East.

The end of this bipolar world gives Europe an opportunity to regain a central place in global decision-making. It did not wait for this event, since since the end of the 1980s, European countries have been seeking to federate. This began with the Single European Act of 1986, which paved the way for the creation of a European market and a common approach to foreign policy, soon followed by the Maastricht Treaty of 1992, establishing the European Union.

Soccer is one of the playgrounds of the time that helps to understand these different upheavals. The 1992 European Championship of Nations in Sweden saw the qualification of the Soviet Union's soccer team, which posed a problem since the USSR officially disappeared on 26 December 1991. It is replaced, at first, by the Community of Independent States (CIS), intergovernmental entity composed of ten former Soviet republics. The former USSR team was allowed to participate in Euro 1992 under the banner of the CIS, the time of a competition, before this team disappeared to make way for the national teams of the newly independent countries.

As the last remnant of the Soviet Empire prepares to play its final soccer tournament, the Balkan region is ablaze with the breakup of Yugoslavia. This federation of multi-ethnic republics was created in 1945. After following the Soviet communist model for a time, the Federal Republic broke with the USSR and maintained a policy of neutrality during the Cold War. It was thanks to the leadership of Tito, the leader of Yugoslavia, that the country managed to escape from Stalin's influence. This leader was to federate Yugoslavia in the strongest possible way, describing it as a federation "composed of six republics, five nations, four languages, three religions, two alphabets and a single party. When he died in 1980, after 35 years in power, the Yugoslav structure began to crumble with the rise of nationalism in the various federated republics, which had long been held in check by the central government.

The collapse of the USSR accelerated the demands for greater autonomy of peoples, particularly in Eastern Europe, where many communist regimes, satellites of Moscow, were overthrown. Yugoslavia was not exempt, with the declaration of independence of two of its federated republics in 1991, Slovenia and Croatia. The Yugoslav state retaliated quickly and the Balkan wars began. While the conflict with Slovenia lasted only ten days, the wars in Croatia and Bosnia lasted for a long time, because Slobodan Milošević's Republic of Serbia wished to integrate the Serbian minorities of these countries into its territory in an offensive manner. It is the conflict against Bosnia that causes the exclusion of the Yugoslav soccer team from the Euro 1992.

The cause? Following the recognition of Bosnia's independence by the international community on April 6, 1992, Yugoslavia counterattacked and bombed the Bosnian capital, Sarajevo. The United Nations sanctions were not long in coming, with the vote of resolution 757 on May 30, 1992. This resolution included a wide range of sanctions, including the obligation for UN member states to prevent the participation of athletes representing the Federal Republic of Yugoslavia in sporting events on their territory. The next day, on May 31, 1992, the FIFA emergency committee immediately decided to suspend the Yugoslavian federation and, in agreement with UEFA, to exclude its national team from the European Nations Championship, which was to begin on June 10 in Sweden.

Ten days before the opening of the competition, it was learned that one of the main favorites will not participate in this great soccer festival. A blow to the team, which then has in its ranks a significant number of players who won the 1991 European

3. When geopolitics reshuffles the cards at Euro 1992

Champion Clubs' Cup with Red Star Belgrade: Siniša Mihajlović, Robert Prosinečki, Dejan Savićević or Darko Pančev, among others. Despite a golden generation, the Yugoslav national team at that time began to follow the same path as his country, fragmented by the war. Coach Ivica Osim and captain Faruk Hadžibegić, both Bosnians, have already packed up following the Serbian army's offensive on their homeland.

With Yugoslavia excluded, the second-placed team in their qualifying group, Denmark, took part in Euro 1992. A funny situation, when you know that, at the same time, the Danes voted 50.7% against the Maastricht Treaty, the founding act of the European Union. At the same time, Danish players said yes to one of the main European sports competitions. According to legend, the Danish national team learned the news while the entire team was on vacation. An image that will stick to the players throughout the competition, described as sportsmen who came to Sweden with flip-flops on their feet, wives on their arms and beers in their pockets.

However, this scenario is far from being true. The player Kim Vilfort said: "A week before, we played a game against the CIS and we were 1-1. The internationals who were playing abroad went on vacation. But during the three days that we had for this game, we learned that it was possible to be drafted. We knew that."[6] An announcement that still postpones the plans of Danish coach Richard Møller Nielsen, who planned that summer to redo his kitchen. The Danes then embarked on a commando course of a few days to get back into the rhythm of the competition. Player John Sivebæk remembers "how messy it was. During the first trainings, the team was not in shape. There were a lot of differences between

---

6. GHEMMOUR Chérif, PEDRO Alexandre, "Once upon a time Richard-Moller Niesen and Denmark 1992," *So Foot*, February 2014.

those who had just finished the season and those who had just come back from vacation"[7].

In addition to this truncated preparation, the Danish selection starts from very far: its stars of the time, the brothers Michael and Brian Laudrup, desert the team since 1990 and the choices of the coach are disputed. The *Danish Dynamite*, the nickname of the team, are only a shadow of their former selves. To top it all off, Denmark has inherited the most complicated group. The opponents are France, undefeated in their qualifying matches, England, third in the 1990 World Cup, and Sweden, the host country.

The Danes start their Euro in the worst way. In two games they don't score any goal, manage to get a miraculous draw against England and lose against the Swedish neighbor, on a goal of Tomas Brolin. While France has its destiny in its hands, Les Bleus will be surprised by Denmark. A goal by Lars Elstrup allowed the Danish team to win the match 2-1 and to go straight to the semi-finals.

The fairy tale will continue. In the semi-final, the underdogs face the defending champions, the Netherlands. After a hard-fought battle, the two teams had to go to a penalty shootout to decide the winner. Goalkeeper Peter Schmeichel's save from a shot by Dutch star Marco Van Basten sent the Danish team into the final. In the final match, the opponent was the reigning world champions, Germany. This is not just any German team, as it is the first reunited German team since the fall of the Berlin Wall and the disappearance of the East German team on September 12, 1990. A victory at the Euro would symbolically seal the reunification of Germany, which was proclaimed on October 3, 1990.

However, right from the start of the game it was the not very prolific Danish midfielder, John "Faxe" Jensen, who opened the

---

7. *Ibid.*

scoring with his only shot on target of the tournament! Proof that this goal is exceptional, the midfielder has scored only one goal in 48 appearances before this game. Kim Vilfort finishes the job and allows Denmark to win 2-0. He had to leave his teammates during the competition to be at the bedside of his daughter, suffering from leukemia - he unfortunately lost the fight against the disease a few days later.

On June 26, 1992, in the Gothenburg stadium, the surprise guest, Denmark, won its first ever European Football Championship. As Vilfort points out, Denmark "didn't have the best players, but probably the best team. The team's nonchalance portrayed by the media was just a facade, as captain Lars Olsen reports, "When we were on the field we were focused and serious, but off the field we could have fun and we had fun." The day after the victory, the press headlines read, "Denmark says yes to the Euro." A premonitory title because, after the Edinburgh agreements which will define exceptions for Denmark, a second referendum will take place in 1993. The Danes will say yes to Europe for a second time by accepting to join the European Union.

4.
WHEN EURO 1996 CONTRIBUTED TO CROATIA'S INTERNATIONAL RECOGNITION

In the early 1990s, the wars in Yugoslavia erupted and exacerbated tensions between the Croatian and Serbian populations in that federation. As Croatia sought independence, its soccer team provided an opportunity to promote the future symbols of its sovereignty and to draw international attention to its situation. It culminated in its first participation in an international soccer competition, Euro 1996, before the "team with the chequered flag" created a surprise at the 1998 World Cup in France.

While we have left Denmark on top of Europe, the situation in the Balkans is getting worse. In the early 1990s, relations between the republics of the Yugoslav federation had been deteriorating for almost a decade. Since the creation of the Federal Republic of Yugoslavia in 1945 after the Second World War, the unity of the country has been maintained with an iron hand by the authoritarian leader Josip Broz Tito. A situation that inspired this metaphor to General de Gaulle: "There are only pieces of wood that hold together [Yugoslavia] because they are tied to a piece of string. The piece of string is Tito. When he is gone, the pieces of wood will scatter."[8] The general was not wrong, since when Tito died in 1980, nationalism reawakened in the six republics of Yugoslavia: Slovenia, Croatia, Bosnia, Serbia, Montenegro and Macedonia.

In the early 1980s, secessionist movements of Albanian minorities emerged in Kosovo, then an autonomous province of Yugoslavia, and in Serbia. Demonstrations were severely repressed. On the Slovenian and Croatian sides, both sides sought greater autonomy within the federation. This was not to the liking of the new strongman of Yugoslavia, President Slobodan Milošević of the Republic of Serbia, who wanted to preserve the unity of the federation while promoting a strong Serbian nationalism. The divorce was finalized in January 1990, when the Croatian and Slovenian delegations left the congress of the League of Communists of Yugoslavia.

A few months later, free elections were scheduled in both countries. In Slovenia, Milan Kučan of the Democratic Reform Party won the election. In Croatia, Franjo Tuđman's Croatian Democratic Union (HDZ) won on May 6, 1990. The atmosphere in Croatian land was more electric than in Slovenia. A majority of Croats wanted Croatia to leave the Yugoslav federation and become a sovereign country. At the same time, many ethnic Serbs living on Croatian soil were opposed to secession and wanted their territory to remain part of Serbia. This tension materialized a week later, on May 13, 1990, during a soccer match between Dinamo Zagreb and Red Star Belgrade. The match, which was to take place in the Maksimir stadium in Zagreb, did not take place. The clashes between the Dinamo supporters, the *Bad Blue Boys*, and the Red Star supporters, the *Delije*, before the match degenerated into riots. After the

---

8. GHEMMOUR Chérif, *Terrain Miné, quand la politique s'immisce dans le soccer*, Hugo Sport, 2013, p. 135.

Serbian fans began to attack their counterparts with shouts of "Zagreb is Serbian" and "We will kill Tuđman"[9], the Croatian fans counterattacked; the stadium was invaded and the match became a real battlefield.

In the midst of this chaos, several Dinamo players remain on the field, including captain Zvonimir Boban, who kicks a Serbian policeman to protect a Croatian fan: "I was there, a public figure ready to risk his life, his career and everything that fame could have brought, for an ideal, a cause: the Croatian cause."[10] A kick that will become a symbol of Croatian resistance against Serbia. The "official" balance sheet is heavy: 138 injured and 147 arrests. This non-match has several consequences: Boban is suspended by the Yugoslav Football Federation for six months, which makes him miss the World Cup in the summer of 1990, depriving the national team of one of its greatest hopes.

More importantly, this confrontation is seen internationally as a symbol of ethnic tensions in Yugoslavia. It is nicknamed "the kick-off of the Balkan war". As Loïc Trégourès, professor of political science and author of the book *Le Football dans le chaos Ygoslave*[11], says, "the incidents at Maksimir served as an illustration of the irreversible nature of the split within Yugoslavia. This match caused the umpteenth spark that fanned the already burning nationalist embers in a tense political context. This meeting remains today for the Croats a founding event of their nation. Thus, at the entrance to the Zagreb stadium, a plaque pays tribute to "the team's supporters who, on this field, started the war against Serbia on May 13, 1990.

---

9. *Ibid*, p. 139.
10. GHEMMOUR Chérif, "The day Boban made his *high kick*," *So Foot*, May 2020.
11. TRÉGOURÈS Loïc, *Football in the Yugoslav chaos*, Non Lieu, 2019.

4. When Euro 1996 contributed to Croatia's international recognition

The Maksimir stadium was again the scene of a demonstration of Croatian nationalism on June 3, 1990. The Yugoslavian team faced the Netherlands in front of hostile tribunes. The Yugoslavian anthem was booed. The spectators chant: "Croatia! Croatia!" The captain at the time, Faruk Hadžibegić even says: "Tonight we are 11 against 20,000."[12]

This stadium still plays a key role in the first representation of Croatia as a national entity. On October 17, 1990, a match took place between a selection of Yugoslav players and the United States team, then on tour in Europe. At least that's what it says on paper. Unofficially, the team present in front of the Americans is indeed a real Croatian team. Whether it's the checkered shirts (the historical coat of arms of the medieval kingdom of Croatia), the anthems played, the banners in the stadium or the match ticket that clearly states "Croatia/USA". The team looks good as it has players selected for the Yugoslavian team, such as midfielder Aljoša Asanović or goalkeeper Dražen Ladić in its ranks. For Croatian soccer, this first match is considered the very first international match of the *Vatreni, the* nickname of the team. The match was followed by another one in December 1990, against Romania, where the young Croatian talents of the time, Zvonimir Boban, Robert Jarni or Davor Šuker, did play. On its side, the FIFA does everything to not officialize these matches and thus not to offend the federation of Yugoslavia.

However, the first official Croatian national team did not see the light of day immediately. On 19 May 1991, Croatia held a referendum in which 93% of voters said yes to independence. The decision was contested by Slobodan Milošević and a month later the People's Army of Yugoslavia invaded the country, which began the Croatian War. A ceasefire intervened in January 1992, with the recognition

---

12. *Ibid*, pp. 58-59.

of Croatia as a sovereign state by the international community. This allowed it to be finally admitted to FIFA and UEFA. However, the late admission did not allow Croatia to participate in the 1994 World Cup qualifiers. The first official match recognized by FIFA took place on September 4, 1994, with a victory over Estonia.

On the battlefield side, after a final Croatian offensive, the war ended with the signing of the Erdut agreement on November 12, 1995. The following year, the Euro 1996 was a great opportunity for this new country to show itself to the whole of Europe. The Croatian national team easily qualified for the competition, finishing in first place in its group, on equal points with Italy, finalists in the last World Cup. These good results were confirmed in the final phase of Euro 1996, as Croatia qualified for the quarterfinals after a convincing 3-0 victory over Denmark, the reigning European champion. The German team stopped the beautiful Croatian adventure, but the important thing was elsewhere: to make Croatia known. As player Igor Štimac said at the time: "We were ambassadors for our country. It was very important that there were Croatian players all over Europe to spread this message, because with us was Croatia and the Croatian flag."[13]

The Croatian national team will be much more talked about two years later, during the 1998 World Cup, where it will shake the host country, France, in the semi-final. They finally lost after a memorable double from Lilian Thuram and finished a surprising third place for their first World Cup. Although this success was a great media showcase for the young country, Croatia will remain diplomatically isolated until the death of its leader, Franjo Tuđman, in 1999, before beginning the steps to be fully integrated into Europe on another field than soccer.

---

13. *Ibid*, pp. 147-148.

II. The geopolitics of Euro 2021

5.
England-Scotland: the "Brexit battle"

On June 18, 2021, the British rivals England and Scotland will face each other in London, in Wembley Stadium, for the first round of Euro 2021. This match will not be a simple game of soccer as relations between Scotland and England have become strained following the Brexit, which marked the exit of the United Kingdom from the European Union in 2020. Since then, the Scots feel aggrieved by this decision and want to leave the British kingdom to join the EU. The duel of this summer could accelerate the process of independence of Scotland...

"My friends in the *Tartan Army* [the nickname for Scotland's fans] are adamant that if Gary McAllister had scored that penalty, Scotland would have won and the whole country would have demanded a vote for independence right away."[14] This is how Mark Perryman, author of the book *Ingerland: Travels with a Football*

---

14. Nakrani Sachin, "Golden goal: Paul Gascoigne for England *v.* Scotland (1996)," *The Guardian*, December 2014.

Nation[15], describes the atmosphere around the England-Scotland game at Euro 1996. History will repeat itself at the 2021 edition of the European Championship, once again highlighting the sporting rivalry between the two countries, which has never been far from the political arena.

The question of Scottish independence will be at the center of the game, as this issue has recently resurfaced. It must be said that, while the United Kingdom did leave the European Union in 2020, the Scots voted more than 60% against Brexit in the 2016 referendum. As a reminder, the United Kingdom is composed of four constituent nations: England, Scotland, Wales and Northern Ireland. The latter three have devolved administrations, which grants them relative autonomy, each with their own government and parliament. This explains why a majority of Scots want to question the decision to leave the EU: why not become a separate state again?

Before turning to the question of independence, it is worthwhile to look back at the origins of this historical-sporting rivalry. England and Scotland have often been the best of enemies in the past. It all began with William the Conqueror's conquest of England in the mid-eighteenth century, when he and his successors were forced to intervene on Scotland's borders to stop attacks on the north. Finally, England and Scotland became two distinct kingdoms during the Middle Ages, alternating between phases of peace and war. The English kingdom sought to acquire the lands of its neighbor during the 13th and 14th centuries, which led to the Scottish wars of independence. These expansionist tendencies forced Scotland to sign a defensive alliance treaty with the kingdom of France in 1295-the "Old Alliance" (*Auld Alliance*).

---

15. PERRYMAN Marc, *Ingerland: Travels With a Football Nation*, Simon & Schuster, 2006.

After a long struggle, James VI, King of Scotland, also became King of England in 1603, creating a personal union between the two kingdoms. Although they shared the same head of state, the two countries were still sovereign and separate. However, a century later, this union was transformed by the Acts of Union in 1707 into a single state, the Kingdom of Great Britain, marking the coming birth of the United Kingdom. Over the centuries, Scottish nationalism grew and eventually Scotland was given greater autonomy with the Scotland Act of 1998, which established a Scottish Parliament for the first time since 1707.

This rivalry was orchestrated throughout the 20th century, particularly through sporting events. This rivalry was particularly evident in football, as England and Scotland were the birthplaces of modern soccer. It was between these two nations that the very first international soccer match took place on November 30, 1872, in the Hamilton Crescent stadium, in Partick, a suburb of Glasgow. Many matches were played to highlight Scottish nationalism against England, with victory often representing a way to dominate the other, as in the Anglo-Scottish wars. As the matches progress, the old antagonisms resurface, since the English team is nicknamed by the Scottish supporters the *Auld Enemy*, in other words the enemy of the old Franco-Scottish alliance of the Middle Ages which preserved the independence.

The Scottish team has impressed in its early days as, although the country is smaller and less populated than its English neighbor, it has recorded 10 wins in the first 16 games against the *Three Lions* team. In all, the two teams have played each other more than 114 times with, for the moment, a slight advantage on the English side with 48 wins, compared to 41 for Scotland, and 25 draws. However, the development of international soccer and the decline of Scottish soccer have reduced the number of head-to-head encounters between these two teams. The soccer rivalry has also shifted, with matches against Germany and Argentina (see Chapter 17) now considered more important for England than the historic rivalry with Scotland. This sporting duel is more common today between the Rose and Thistle teams.

However, some matches in recent decades have brought this rivalry back to life. In particular, the match of June 15, 1996 at Wembley Stadium in London, during the European Championship of Nations. This Euro is organized by England, while the national team is moribund. It comes out of a failed Euro 92 and a non-qualification for the 1994 World Cup. The pressure is clearly on the English side since the press of the time is waiting for the *Three Lions* team to turn the corner. On the side of the fans, the hope is great, as shown by the popular success of the song *It's Coming Home* of the band The Lightning Seeds. The song rekindled the hopes of a nation of soccer fans for the return of a major trophy (the last one was the 1966 World Cup) to the birthplace of the game.

The luck of the draw meant that Britain's best enemies were drawn in the same group for this Euro. Rumors were circulating at the time that UEFA did not want them to be drawn together, for fear that the hot English and Scottish fans would come to blows. The match is already a crucial one for the rest of the competition. Both teams started this Euro with a draw, England against Switzerland and Scotland against the Netherlands. This duel has already all the cutter match because a defeat would eject one of these two teams of the Euro.

In the stands, Wembley Stadium, with its 70,000 spectators, is in meltdown. The Scottish national anthem, *Flower of Scotland,* was completely drowned out by the boos of the fans. With the game hard fought, England striker Alan Shearer broke the deadlock in the 53rd minute. Just 15 minutes later, *Three Lions* defender Tony Adams ran down Scotland striker Gordon Durie. With the entire stadium holding its breath, goalkeeper David Seaman turned Gary McAllister's penalty into a corner. Seconds later, England's counter-attack allowed the whimsical Paul Gascoigne to make a sumptuous sombrero move before crucifying goalkeeper Andy Goram with a right-footed finish. 2-0 for England. A liberation for the whole team and a nice answer from "Gazza", who had been the target of the English tabloids after his extrasporting problems, in particular a drunken trip with several other players during the preparation camp in Hong Kong.

After this match, both British teams can still qualify for the rest of the competition, but Scotland is finally eliminated on goal difference. However, in the last game of the group, England had the fate of their neighbor in their hands, after leading the Netherlands 4-0. A "late" goal by the Dutch team, however, brought the score to 4-1 and eliminated Scotland from the competition. The *Guardian* newspaper reports that, after the match, "England fans were overjoyed when Dutch player Patrick Kluivert scored the goal to deny Scotland a place in the quarter-finals"[16].

This match was not the only notable confrontation between the two teams. England and Scotland met again in a double playoff for Euro 2000 on November 13 and 17, 1999 in a duel dubbed by the press as "the Battle of Britain. The tension was high as the first leg, at Hampden Park in Glasgow, was the first game the two teams had played in Scotland for almost ten years. England won 2-0, thanks to midfielder Paul Scholes, while the battle between the fans

---

16. GIBBONS Michael, "The cultural resonance of Euro 96," *The Guardian*, July 2016.

around the stadium raged. The return match in London made the *Three Lions* doubt, the Scottish team trying everything, but finally winning only with a 1-0. This was not enough to prevent England from qualifying for Euro 2000 - for the record, they will go out in the first round.

Although the two teams have met since then, the June 18, 2021 match at London's Wembley Stadium will be the first duel between England and Scotland in a major soccer competition since 2016. A duel that has everything to be the next "Battle of Britain". Will the outcome of the match influence the question of Scottish independence? The subject is in any case hot. It is true that the last referendum on this subject had seen the no camp win on September 18, 2014 with 55% of the votes. In 2021, in the post-Brexit context, the deal is quite different.

Scotland's political powers are already organizing themselves accordingly. On January 25, Nicola Sturgeon, leader of the Scottish Nationalist Party (SNP), unveiled her roadmap to independence: "I want a legal referendum, which is why I will appeal to the authority of the Scottish people in May. And if they give me that authority, I will act on it." [17]

It must be said that despite the trade agreement found following the Brexit, Scotland feels aggrieved on many points, especially fishing. The Brexit complicates the exports of this country, which is the first European producer of salmon, and which is now deprived of the benefits of the European market. If Scotland's national team wins this summer, it will be interesting to see if a sporting event of this magnitude can precipitate a referendum and act, after the European Union, as a new divorce for the United Kingdom.

---

17. Brooks Libby, "Sturgeon: SNP will hold Scottish independence vote if it wins in May," *The Guardian*, January 2021.

6.

NORTH MACEDONIA:
A HISTORIC PARTICIPATION IN EURO 2021

In 2021, a newcomer will take part in its very first Euro soccer tournament: North Macedonia. A historic step, because it is the first time that this young nation will take part in this competition. This will integrate the Balkan country a little more into the big European sporting family, before, why not, joining the European Union.

"The dream has come true."[18] This is how Macedonian soccer star Goran Pandev, who scored the only goal in North Macedonia's victory over Georgia on November 12, 2020, put it. This success has indeed allowed the team to participate in the Euro. It is simply the first time in its young history that the Macedonian team has qualified for a major international soccer tournament. This Euro 2021 will be an opportunity to highlight a country that has the distinction of being new on the international scene, since Northern Macedonia is called so recently, following the resolution of a diplomatic dispute

18. Editor, "Football: a united North Macedonia celebrates its qualification for the Euro", *The Balkan Courier*, November 2020.

with Greece. To better understand why this change occurred, it is necessary to go back a bit.

Macedonia is above all known thanks to Alexander the Great. Crowned king of Macedonia at the age of 20, victorious in many battles, he conquered a huge empire in ancient times, from Greece to the gates of India. In the course of history, Macedonia was a region with variable geometry and lost its prestige, until it lost its independence. At the beginning of the 20th century, the modern territory of Macedonia, under Ottoman domination, was then the object of covetousness between Albania, Bulgaria, Greece and Serbia. Several movements pushed for Macedonian independence, but between the beginning of the 20th century and the Second World War, this territory passed under Bulgarian and then Serbian domination, before being integrated into the kingdom of Yugoslavia.

In December 1944, the Anti-Fascist Assembly for the Liberation of the Macedonian People (ASNOM) founded the first Socialist Republic of Macedonia, which was later integrated into the six republics of the federal Yugoslav state. It was in the 1980s that the unity of Yugoslavia began to crumble. It must be said that at that time the Yugoslav state lost its historic leader, Tito, whose authoritarianism had helped to contain the various nationalisms of the federal republic (see Chapter 4). The gradual collapse of the USSR and its Eastern bloc in 1991 led to this process within Yugoslavia. The successive declarations of independence by the former socialist republics of Slovenia and Croatia precipitated the collapse of the federation. Northern Macedonia followed suit and held a referendum in which over 95 per cent of the votes were in favour of self-determination. On September 8, 1991, the Republic of Macedonia was proclaimed.

To fully integrate into the international scene, the new country is trying to join the United Nations quickly. It is from this moment that *the* problem intervenes: the name of the country is disputed by Greece. If there is such a dispute, it is because the Greek state claims the exclusive use of the term Macedonia for the northern province of its territory. A ground and a name, as we saw, charged with history and carrying the myth of Alexander the Great. For Greece, if a state bears the name of Macedonia, it means that the integrity of Greek territory is threatened.

A first solution was found as Northern Macedonia joined the UN in 1993, under the provisional name of the Former Yugoslav Republic of Macedonia (FYROM). This compromise did not suit Greece, which imposed a blockade on Macedonian territory from 1994. The sanctions are finally lifted in September 1995, after a conciliation under the aegis of the UN. Macedonia changes different aspects of its Constitution and some elements of its flag to remove any ambiguity with the Greek claims. The conflict over the name is finally resolved much later. On June 17, 2018, FYROM and Greece signed the Prespa agreement, which opened a new era for the Macedonian country. It is officially renamed the Republic of North Macedonia on February 12, 2019. The end of the diplomatic dispute allows the lifting of the Greek diplomatic veto. A boon for this "new country", which can now join the largest international organizations. This is the case with the Euro-Atlantic alliance of NATO on 27 March 2020. And why not soon the European Union? Northern Macedonia has been an official candidate for membership since 2004, and its government has set this goal as a strategic priority.

This international spotlight will continue since, as we said, the soccer team of Macedonia validated its entry ticket for its first Euro on November 12, 2020, with a victory over Georgia. A historic qualification for a country that is more used to seeing its basketball or handball teams in the spotlight. Since joining FIFA and UEFA in 1994, the Macedonian national team, nicknamed the *Crveni Lavovi* ("Red Lions"), has hardly ever been in the news. The Euro is thus a great opportunity to highlight a small country of 25,000 km≤ and 2 million inhabitants.

The qualification against Georgia also allowed the Macedonian population to gather around the common national symbol that a soccer team can constitute. The scenes of jubilation were numerous throughout Northern Macedonia, and the country's anthem resounded in the streets of the capital Skopje. Images of unity that are good for a country that has experienced stormy relations with the Albanian minority of its population. It must be said that the Balkan wars of the 1990s increased tensions between Macedonians of Slavic origin and Macedonians of Albanian origin. The war in Kosovo led to the immigration of nearly 360,000 Albanian refugees to the country. In 2001, former fighters from that war launched a guerrilla war with the aim of annexing the Albanian regions of Macedonia (the Albanian minority represents about 25% of the Macedonian population) and integrating them into the new Kosovar territory. International mediation brought the conflict to an end with the signing of the Ohrid agreements on August 13, 2001. These agreements gave greater political power and cultural recognition to the Albanian minority, and made Albanian one of the country's two official languages, along with Macedonian.

The soccer success of North Macedonia has brought the country together across differences, as half of the players on the national team are from the Albanian minority. As Goran Pandev says, "We won for our people and for all of us. This message of unity is also relayed by the country's Prime Minister, Zoran Zaev: "Macedonians, Albanians, Turks... under the same shirt, under the same flag, for the common homeland."[19] This is the proof that from now on the soccer team of North Macedonia will have more than a sporting role to play during the Euro. It will have a role of ambassador of the country, to convey positive values about the country, far from the ethnic conflicts of the region.

A good run at the European Championship this summer could further put this little-known territory on the map, just like Iceland did at the 2016 edition. As Darko Pančev, former Yugoslavian and Macedonian soccer glory, says, "This generation of players has a unique opportunity to succeed and play against the best teams in Europe." Macedonian soccer has the wind in its sails, because even if the 37-year-old star Goran Pandev is going towards the end of his career, players like Eljif Elmas, Enis Bardhi or Ezgjan Alioski are playing in the top 5 of European leagues.

Northern Macedonia is still fighting for its full integrity, as Bulgaria recently put forward a historical and linguistic dispute to justify its veto in the talks between the Macedonian country and the European Union. Will the game of football allow North Macedonia to gain full recognition on the international stage? It is difficult to predict. In any case, the Euro and its thousands of television viewers will be a great window of opportunity to showcase the flag of this young Balkan nation.

---

19. *Ibid.*

7. Turkey:
Soccer in the service of Erdoğan

As the Turkish team will play the opening match of this Euro 2021, the links between the political power of Turkish President Recep Tayyip Erdoğan *and the round ball are increasingly present. It must be said that* Erdoğan *and his party, the AKP, have been investing in Turkey's king of sports, almost a "second religion," for nearly ten years. These investments serve above all to legitimize a power that is tipping more and more into authoritarianism. And it inspires other regimes, such as Viktor Orbán's Hungary, whose national team will play against Germany and France this summer.*

Euro 2020 has been postponed by one year but the opening match remains the same as it will oppose Turkey to Italy on June 11, 2021 in Rome. An interesting match to watch both on and off the field, because for some years the Turkish national team has been a real showcase for the country, but also in some ways a relay of the political regime of the Turkish president, Recep Tayyip Erdoğan. In France, we remember in particular the match between Les Bleus and the Turkish team on October 14, 2019, during which the Turkish players celebrated their goal by performing a military salute. A gesture that they dedicated at the time "to the valiant soldiers, military and fellow citizens fallen as martyrs", in reference to the conflict between Turkish and Kurdish forces.

It must be said that, for some years now, President Erdoğan has sought to reassert Turkey's territorial integrity, thus extinguishing all forms of regionalism. This includes the Kurds, a predominantly Sunni Muslim people of about 40 million who live in the border areas of Turkey, Syria, Iraq and Iran. A national minority in all these states, the Kurds have for years been demanding a state, Kurdistan, corresponding to their settlement area. The Syrian conflict has considerably strained the situation since the Kurds are actively involved in the fight against Daech. This situation worries the central power in Ankara, which fears the creation of an autonomous Kurdish region serving as a rear base for the operations of the Kurdistan Workers' Party (PKK), considered a terrorist organization by Turkey. On October 9, 2019, Erdoğan launched the "Source of Peace" operation to restore Turkish control in this region deemed secessionist.

The gesture of support from the Turkish players in fact testifies above all to the strong bond that unites the Turkish army with its people. A gesture more patriotic than a real support to Erdoğan's policy, so important is the relationship of the Turkish people with their army. Despite numerous calls for a boycott of Turkey's matches at the time, UEFA did not equate these gestures with provocation. Will the situation change if such celebrations are repeated in UEFA's flagship competition, the Euro?

Also note that in addition to the strong political messages that the Turkish national soccer team can distill, Erdoğan's political power has been investing massively in the sport since the early 2010s. A way for the Turkish president to use the round ball to legitimize his power. To understand this approach, one must remember that soccer is a second religion in Turkey and that stadiums and clubs are real institutions, sometimes places of counter-power. As Jean-Baptiste Guégan, a professor of the geopolitics of sport, explains, "[there] has always been a real link between soccer and politics in Turkey; it is the only place in the public arena where there is a kind of army in spikes that represents the country."[20]

Therefore, in 2014, people close to Erdoğan's political party, the AKP, began to invest in Turkish soccer by buying the Istanbul municipality club, Istanbul Büyükşehir Belediyesi Spor Kulübün, which would soon be renamed Istanbul Başakşehir. If it changes its name in 2014, it is because the team moves to the Başakşehir district, an Islamoconservative district created from scratch in the 1990s by the then mayor of Istanbul, one Recep Tayyip Erdoğan. According to Dağhan Irak, a senior lecturer at the University of Huddersfield and author of the book *Football Fandom, Protest and Democracy: Supporter Activism in Turkey (Critical Research in soccer)*[21], "[the] Başakşehir neighborhood totally reflects Erdoğan's strategy for this club. He created this neighborhood in the 1990s when he felt that the Islamist lifestyle was dominated by the modern, secular lifestyle of Istanbul. He presented it as the epicenter of his cultural project to replace the city's former cultural centers, Beyoğlu, Beşiktaş and Kadiköy."[22]

---

20. CULTURES MONDE (Florian Delorme's program), "Le sport, arme de séduction massive (2/4). Turkish soccer; a tool of nationalism, ferment of contestation", *France Culture*, January 2020.
21. IRAQ Dağhan, *Football Fandom Protest and Democracy. Supporter activism in Turkey*, Routledge, 2019.
22. HOUEIX Romain, "Football: the Başakşehir, a Turkish champion who owes a lot to Erdoğan," *France 24*, July 2020.

Thus, Erdogan and his party invest in an extremely popular sport and make a club the showcase of his Islamoconservative political regime. The links between the AKP, Erdoğan and the club do not end there as Istanbul Başakşehir plays in orange, the colors of the party. In addition, the Turkish president dons the boots for the opening of the club's new stadium on July 26, 2014. At the end of the match, Erdoğan scored a hat-trick and his jersey number, 12, was retired from the team! This is another opportunity to highlight the politician's past as a semi-professional footballer, to overexploit the image of a sports president. Let's add that the new Fatih-Terim stadium (named after an illustrious Turkish coach) was built by Kalyon Group, a conglomerate close to the government, which manages the construction of state infrastructures.

This gradual takeover of Turkish soccer goes hand in hand with the political rise, since 2010, of the AKP and Erdoğan, who, like the majority of politicians, have clearly understood the importance of the unifying power of football. In particular, the match-fixing scandal in the Turkish league in 2011 accelerated these changes. Another event pushed Erdoğan's regime to reform soccer: the waves of popular protests against the planned destruction of Taksim Gezi Park in Istanbul in 2013. The harsh repression orchestrated by the power against the demonstrators leads to numerous protests in the country, which expand to other demands: freedom of the press, freedom of expression, defense of secularism - undermined by the Erdoğan government. At the center of the demonstrations in Istanbul; there is a fringe of Beşiktaş supporters, the *Carsi*. They were soon joined by ultrasupporters of the two big rival Istanbul clubs, Galatasaray and Fenerbaçhe, to form the short-lived Istanbul United movement. After these demonstrations, stadiums and fan groups were seen as hotbeds of protest. More control was introduced, which led to the creation of the electronic ticketing system Passolig. These measures were aimed at limiting the role of ultras in the stadiums, but also as an attempt by the regime to dethrone the three big clubs of Istanbul, although they keep a close relationship with the power, as today all clubs in the country.

Istanbul Başakşehir (IB) struggles to federate around itself, while the clubs of Beşiktaş, Galatasaray or Fenerbaçhe know the crowds on match days, with more than 30,000 people - the average IB audience does not exceed 3,000 people. Federating the population around this regime-sponsored soccer club takes time. Time that the AKP and Erdogan have, who now enjoy broad support from Turkish soccer, while most of the key positions are in the hands of people close to the political party. Thus, Erdoğan may be tempted to rely on the patriotism of the Turkish national team to link his action to it and establish his legitimacy. A Turkish victory against other great nations could represent much more than a sporting success.

This is the model that Hungarian Prime Minister Viktor Orbán is trying to replicate. In office since 2010, he is one of the leaders of this new wave of authoritarian regimes in European Union countries. Under his leadership, Hungary has experienced a democratic retreat, tilting toward authoritarianism. Orbán's populism and euroscepticism have drawn criticism from the EU in recent years. That is why the Hungarian head of state is looking for ways to legitimize his actions and his power. Sport can be one of them, especially *through* the Hungarian national team, which is participating in Euro 2021.

Soccer and Hungary share a long history, marked in particular by the glorious past of its national team in the 1950s, the "Magyar Golden Eleven", led by Ferenc Puskás. Orbán relies on this heritage to assert the country's nationalism. In his home village of Felcsút, with a population of only 1,800, he has created a brand new soccer club called Puskás Akadémia FC. The club has received 192 million euros of public money *through* a government program to finance Hungarian sports. Viktor Orbán reminds us that "soccer enabled Hungary to defeat the team of an occupying power [the USSR], so soccer should be treated as part of culture and history"[23]. The aim of this club and soccer academy is to train players who can improve the image of the Hungarian team (which is currently ranked 37th in the FIFA rankings).

We must not hide the fact that this Euro 2021 will be an opportunity for Orbán's Hungary to confront political opponents (Germany, France), and therefore to stage this rivalry.

---

23. KATALENIC Antun, "On the Football Pitch, Orban woos Hungarians abroad," *Balkan Insight,* January 2019.

8.

Russia - Ukraine: the unlikely match

Since 2014 and the annexation of the Ukrainian peninsula of Crimea by Russia, relations between the two eastern countries have been tense. So much so that UEFA, the European soccer organization, has banned the two national teams from meeting. While the political situation is still blocked, both teams are present at Euro 2021 and the chance of the final stages of the competition could, why not? let this "forbidden match" take place.

The 16th edition of the European Championship of Nations will take place this summer, with 24 national teams present. However, the health situation should change the format of this competition. The former president of UEFA, Michel Platini, decided in 2012 that for the 60 years of the Euro in 2020, this illustrious European tournament would be held in 12 cities in 12 different countries. Namely: London, Munich, Rome, St. Petersburg, Baku, Amsterdam, Dublin, Bilbao, Budapest, Glasgow, Copenhagen and Bucharest. For Platini, this format would benefit "the development of many countries that would never have had the opportunity to have the Euro, to build eight stadiums that cost a fortune. They [have] the chance to organize the Euro once in their lives"[24]. The organization of the tournament throughout Europe, which is likely to be disrupted right up to the last moment, has caused a lot of talk and has led to some hazardous situations in the drawing of lots for the six groups of the competition.

This draw has, indeed, not much to do with chance since it is subject to many constraints. First of all, there is the UEFA coefficient, which ranks the various national teams according to their results. Then there is the host country criterion, which means that the national teams whose country is hosting the competition must be in a separate group in order to play in their stadium. Finally, the geopolitical criterion is taken into account by UEFA, since some teams are simply banned from playing each other due to political tensions between their countries. This resulted, for example, in Belgium knowing before the Euro 2021 draw that they would be in a group with Denmark and Russia.

How is such a situation possible? In part, as we said, because of the geopolitical criterion. Teams from Russia and Ukraine, qualified for the competition, simply cannot be in the same group. This UEFA prohibition already affected the qualifying phase of the Euro, where, for example, Kosovo could not play against Bosnia-Herzegovina and Serbia. These provisions also affect the matches between Armenia and Azerbaijan or between Gibraltar and Spain. Cases that we will study later in this book.

However, the Ukraine-Russia case goes even further since, since July 17, 2014, this ban concerns all matches between Russian and Ukrainian national teams, or clubs in UEFA competitions: "In view of the current political situation, the Russian federation and the

---

24. Deloraine Hugo, "Euro 2020: Platini defends his Euro in 12 countries," *World Eleven,* November 2019.

Ukrainian federation have expressed their concern about security in case Russian and Ukrainian teams should play each other in UEFA competitions."[25] This case is explained by the fact that Russia has never truly accepted Ukraine's independence.

Both countries have an ancient history, from the ninth to the eleventh century, the state of Kiev, which covers the current Ukraine, is the first state of the Eastern Slavs before the imposition of the Grand Duchy of Muscovy, which will become Russia. Most of Ukraine was part of the Russian Empire in the 17th and 18th centuries, but it was not independent until 1918-1920, when it became part of the USSR. The collapse of the Soviet bloc allowed Ukraine to break away from its imposing neighbor and become independent in 1991. But the influence of the new Russian state remained very present in the country, due to the strong presence of Russian minorities, and in Ukrainian political life. 2005 was a crucial year: Ukrainians voted for pro-Russian Viktor Yanukovych in the presidential election. This result provoked a series of demonstrations, called the "Orange Revolution", which led to the cancellation of the election and, finally, the election of a new president, Viktor Yushchenko. Russia was not happy with this situation, as Yushchenko wanted to detach himself from Moscow's influence in order to obtain eventual membership in the European Union and NATO.

In 2010, Yanukovych regained power through the ballot box and began a rapprochement with his Russian ally, which is why his government refused to sign rapprochement agreements with the European Union in 2013. A crisis then erupted, leading to the Ukrainian revolution of Maïdan in 2014, followed by a change of governance and direction at the head of the country. Very quickly,

---

25. AFP dispatch, "UEFA: no matches between Russian and Ukrainian clubs," July 17, 2014.

8. Russia - Ukraine: the unlikely match

tensions caused scuffles between the predominantly Russian-speaking territories of the southeast of the country and the new central power in Kiev. A civil war broke out between pro-Russian separatists and the Ukrainian army in the Donbass region in the east of the country. On March 11, 2014, Crimea, where a large part of the Russian fleet resides in Sevastopol, proclaims its independence. Then, following a referendum, Crimea is attached to Russia on March 18, 2014. These events are condemned by Ukraine and a large part of the international community. Thus, on March 27, 2014, the UN General Assembly voted the resolution 68/262 on "the territorial integrity of Ukraine", the majority of countries contesting the attachment of Crimea to Russia.

For nearly six years, Ukraine has been seeking to regain its entire territory. UEFA has not reviewed its ban on matches between the two countries as there are recurring clashes, as was the case in November 2018 in the Sea of Azov. Until the main dividing point in Crimea is resolved between Ukraine and Russia, it does not seem feasible to see their national teams meet on a soccer field. On the Crimean side, the territory is between two waters, as evidenced by the situation of its local soccer. In late 2014, Crimean clubs wanted to join the Russian Football Federation, which welcomed them with open arms. Ukraine contested this move, and in December 2014, the European body UEFA banned Crimean teams from playing in the Russian league: "Crimea will be considered a 'special zone' until further notice."[26] In order not to let a Crimean soccer that had become stateless die, UEFA approved the creation of the Crimean Premier League, a league specific to the peninsula, under the aegis of its own federation. The league remains isolated, however, as it

---

26. AFP Dispatch, "UEFA bans Crimean clubs from Russian competitions," December 4, 2014.

cannot participate in European Cup matches. As a result, the clubs in the region are in total disarray, so much so that Crimea has decided to create a national soccer team to get out of this situation and have real autonomy from Russia. Similarly, the Faroe Islands, although a Danish territory, are full members of UEFA and can play under their national colors.

Therefore, the leaders of the Crimean Football Union plan to become members of UEFA in 2018, appealing to the precedent of the official recognition in May 2016 of the Kosovo team. Although for Russian sports expert Valery Fedoreev, this argument is too weak: "Kosovo is an independent state recognized by the majority of UN member countries. The situation in Crimea is very different."[27] Different because, on paper, Crimea is a secessionist territory of Ukraine, not recognized by the international community, while in fact the region is under Russian control. Since the international community does not recognize Crimea as an autonomous territory or as Russian territory, it seems unlikely that UEFA will respond favorably to the various demands of Crimean soccer.

Since then, Ukraine still contests the Russian invasion while Vladimir Putin is trying to attach this region of Crimea to the rest of its territory with the construction of a bridge. On the Ukrainian side, a rapprochement is being made with the European Union as, on January 1, 2016, Ukraine joined the free trade area that aims to modernize and develop the economy, governance and the rule of law.

As long as this issue remains unresolved, Ukraine and Russia will remain at odds. Even if the UN raises its voice by regularly calling on Moscow to end its temporary occupation, the solution will only come from a political agreement between the two countries. Soccer

27. Mosko Alexei, "Crimea wants to become a full-fledged soccer nation," *Russia Beyond,* November 2016.

could be one of the first areas of discussion since, even if the Russian and Ukrainian teams cannot play each other, the chance of the Euro 2021 finals, from the round of 16 onwards, could give substance to such a scenario.

III. The impossible matches

9.
The case of Kosovo

Independent since 2008, Kosovo continues to see its existence as a sovereign state questioned. It must be said that this Balkan territory has a complex history with its neighbor, Serbia, which is doing everything possible with its allies to prevent it from being recognized internationally. Although its entry into the UN seems to be blocked today, Kosovo does not lack resources. The Kosovar state does not hesitate to use its national soccer team to try to break down the political barriers of this diplomatic imbroglio.

In the previous chapter, we mentioned the case of the "impossible match" between the soccer teams of Ukraine and Russia. This is not the only confrontation that UEFA wants to avoid at all costs. It is also the case of the Kosovo team that cannot play against Serbia and Bosnia-Herzegovina in an official match. It must be said that the Kosovar issue raises a lot of tension with its neighbors in the Balkan region. Why is this so? The existence of the former Yugoslavian state has been disputed since its declaration of independence in 2008. Recognized by FIFA and UEFA, but not by the UN, Kosovo uses soccer as a diplomatic channel to assert its existence and to fully enter the game of nations.

What is Kosovo? It is a territory in Central Europe of 10,887 km², landlocked between Albania, Northern Macedonia, Montenegro and Serbia. The history of Kosovo is a complex story, intimately linked to that of its Albanian and Serbian neighbors. From 1878 and the Congress of Nations in Berlin, the Kingdom of Serbia became independent and was entrusted with the territory of present-day Kosovo. It must be said that this land is associated in the history of the Serbian imagination, the battle of Kosovo Polje, June 15, 1389, or Battle of the Field of Blackbirds "which saw the Ottoman Empire and a coalition of Christian princes, including Serbia. It is the foundation of the myth that Kosovo is the cradle of the Serbian nation.

Later, during the Second World War, Kosovo became part of Albania, which was then controlled by fascist Italy. After the war and the creation of the Eastern bloc under the aegis of the USSR, Tito, the Yugoslav communist leader, intended to create a federation of the various Balkan countries, the Socialist Federal Republic of Yugoslavia. This did not please the leader of the USSR, Stalin, who wanted to control all the countries of Eastern Europe. In 1948, the rupture was consummated between the Soviet and Yugoslav states. The relations were broken. Albania joined the great cohort of "people's democracies" while Kosovo was integrated into Yugoslavia as an autonomous province.

However, after the death of the authoritarian Tito in 1980, the first nationalist demonstrations broke out in this large federation. Kosovo, with a majority of Albanians, wanted to become a republic in its own right. Yugoslavia's communist rulers, influenced by the Republic of Serbia and its leader Slobodan Milošević, disagreed and harshly suppressed the riots. With the collapse of the USSR, from 1989 onwards, many Eastern Bloc nations fought for their independence, which caused a snowball effect within the Yugoslav Federal

Republic: several of its members demanded independence. This was the case for Slovenia, Croatia and Bosnia. Slobodan Milošević's Serbia tried to save what was left of the federation by force, which triggered the bloody Yugoslav wars. The Dayton Agreement of 1995 put an end to this inter-ethnic fighting and to the end of the great federation of Yugoslavia, which is now composed only of Serbia, Montenegro and Kosovo.

However, this new republic was not finished with the war, since there was now a desire for independence in the south. A new war broke out in 1998 in Kosovo between Albanian separatists and Serbian forces, killing more than 13,000 people and causing massive emigration. NATO's intervention in 1999 put an end to the armed conflict and the repressive regime of Slobodan Milošević.

Kosovo remained a territory with an undetermined status until 2007. It was not until then that former Finnish President Martti Ahtisaari, who was overseeing negotiations between the Serbian and Kosovar governments, submitted a proposal to the United Nations Security Council to grant Kosovo the status of an independent state. Russia, a permanent member of the Council, vetoed the resolution because it believed that independence would violate the principle of territorial unity of its Serbian ally. However, the provisional parliament of Kosovo did not wait for UN approval and unilaterally declared its independence on February 17, 2008.

Since then, there has been a long diplomatic struggle to have Kosovo recognized as such. As of September 4, 2020, 98 of the 193 members of the United Nations have recognized this independence, including the United States, France and Germany. Although present in several international organizations (IMF, World Bank), the new Kosovar state is not part of one of the most important, the UN, because of the Russian veto. Russia and Serbia are not the only countries fiercely opposed to the recognition of Kosovo as a state. This is also the case for China and Spain, for whom recognition of Kosovo's independence would send a positive signal to the strong regionalist demands within their borders (Tibet and Xinjiang in China, the Basque Country and Catalonia in Spain). As for Serbia, it has been conducting a major diplomatic campaign since 2017 to get some states to limit visas for Kosovar nationals and to revoke their decision to recognize Kosovo. Since March 2, 2020, and the revocation of Sierra Leone, they are 15 countries that have taken this path.

In addition to this diplomatic conflict, a territorial conflict persists between Serbia and Kosovo. The northern part of the Kosovo territory, with a Serb majority, does not recognize the authority of Pristina, the capital of Kosovo, but that of Belgrade. This can cause dramatic situations, as when, at the end of 2018, the Kosovar government introduced a tax on all products imported from Serbia and Bosnia and Herzegovina, countries with a large Serbian minority. This tax heavily affects the Serbian population present in northern Kosovo. To avoid a humanitarian disaster in July 2019, Pristina is sending food products there, but, fearing that they will be poisoned by the Albanians, the local Serbs refuse to buy them.

These diplomatic and territorial tensions explain why a match between Kosovo and Serbia or Kosovo and Bosnia-Herzegovina, under the auspices of UEFA, cannot take place. For fear that the battle on the pitch would lead to a conflict. The memory of the famous match between Dinamo Zagreb and Red Star Belgrade on May 13, 1990, at the Maksimir stadium, remains in the memory. For the press of the time, it was the start of the Yugoslavian wars. Although the reality is more complex (see Chapter 4), the outbursts at this match had crossed borders and highlighted the eminently political role of soccer in the Balkans.

Football played an important role in the Kosovar resistance during the 1990s, as explained more precisely in Loïc Trégourès' book, *Le Football dans le chaos Ygoslave*[28]. It is a means of resisting Serbia, of structuring Kosovar civil society and of fighting for independence. It continues to be used since 2008, since Kosovo uses sport to exist on the international scene. The sports representation allows to put forward the Kosovar nation through its colors and its flag. Kosovo is, for example, a member of the International Olympic Committee (IOC) since 2014, which gives it the opportunity to send a delegation of athletes to the Rio Olympics in 2016. On this occasion, the judoka Majlinda Kelmendi won the Olympic gold and allowed the Kosovar anthem, "Europe", to be played in front of billions of viewers who followed the competition.

In soccer, it is a longer way to reach the queen of competitions, the World Cup. It has already been a battle to become a member of UEFA and FIFA. It is done since May 3, 2016, when 28 of the 54 members of the UEFA congress voted in favor of Kosovo's membership. FIFA membership followed, which now allows the *Dardanians*, the nickname of the Kosovo team, to take part in the World Cup qualifiers as well as those of the Euro. An essential recognition as soccer is an important part of the Kosovar nation, and a feat made possible thanks to former player Fadil Vokrri, president of the Football Federation of Kosovo, unfortunately passed away in 2018[29].

With only 2 million inhabitants, Kosovo is far from being ridiculous on the soccer planet as the team has strung together an

---

28. TRÉGOURÈS Loïc, *op. cit.* - chap. 10, p. 175.
29. LEFEVRE Florian, "Fadil Vokrri", *So Foot*, June 2020.

9. The case of Kosovo

impressive 15-game unbeaten streak between March 24, 2018 and September 10, 2019. It has risen from 190th in the FIFA rankings in 2016 to 117th today. The fact that the team is progressing so quickly, and is already no longer a "small team," is largely because it relies on its strong diaspora, that is, the dispersion of its community after the war and still today across Europe. There are, for example, about 200,000 Kosovars in Switzerland, or 10% of the current population of Kosovo. The national team is therefore composed in large part of players who were not born in the country or who have already played at the international level under other colors.

Above all, players of Albanian origin, and therefore close to the Kosovar identity, mobilized long before 2016 for this team to exist on the ball. In 2012, the Albanian international Lorik Cana, as well as the Swiss players Granit Xhaka, Valon Behrami and Xherdan Shaqiri, all of Kosovar Albanian origin, wrote to FIFA to request that Kosovo be allowed to play official friendly matches, an initiative supported by many other footballers. In 2016, FIFA allowed players to play for the *Dardanians*, after having worn the jersey of another selection.

This is not the case for the Swiss Shaqiri and Xhaka since the new regulations of FIFA. However, the two companions are attached to Kosovo. In fact, they celebrated, during the victory of Switzerland against Serbia at the 2018 World Cup, the goals of their team by linking their hands with their thumbs. A gesture that has nothing trivial since it symbolizes the two-headed eagle, the rallying sign of the Albanians. FIFA fined the players, which led to the opening of an online kitty on the Kosovar and Albanian side. The Minister of Trade and Industry of Kosovo at the time also participated by donating 1,500 euros, his entire salary. For the current coach of Kosovo, the Swiss Bernard Challandes, it is less and less complicated to convince players to come and play under the blue and yellow colors, because there is a dynamic around the selection. Such enthusiasm could have allowed Kosovo to be part of the Euro 2021, but a defeat against its neighbor, Northern Macedonia, has postponed this goal.

Despite its contested status, and the impossible matches against Serbia and Bosnia-Herzegovina, soccer remains the best tool for recognition and hope for a relatively poor territory with high emigration. It is not for nothing that the Kosovar government set up a ministry for the diaspora in 2011. Participation in an international soccer competition would highlight the situation of Kosovo, which, like Serbia, wants to join the European Union for a better future.

The issue is still pending, of course, as some EU members do not officially recognize Kosovo. This is the case of Spain, which recently created a controversy when its soccer federation questioned the existence of the territory. On the occasion of a World Cup 2022 qualifying match on March 31, the Spanish Football Federation announced that its national team was playing "the territory of Kosovo" and that the team could not display the symbols of the Kosovar nation. Kosovo was quick to challenge this, threatening not to play the match. Without doubt for fear of being excluded by FIFA, Spain has reversed and the match finally took place normally. Proof that there is still a long way to go for Kosovo and that soccer plays an eminently political role in its recognition.

10.

GIBRALTAR-SPAIN

In the south of Spain, Gibraltar, a "rock" of about 6 km², is the object of one of the oldest diplomatic conflicts, between Spain and the United Kingdom. A conflict that has taken another turn since 2013, since Gibraltar won its fight against its Spanish neighbor to be able to participate in official soccer matches through its national team. Madrid is not about to endorse the situation, and is still trying to establish its sovereignty over the territory.

As we mentioned in the previous chapter, Spain remains opposed to the recognition of Kosovo. This is not the only geo-politico-football situation on which Madrid is stuck. There is another one, which concerns a smaller territory, a "rock". We are not talking about Monaco, but about an enclave that generates a lot of tension: Gibraltar. Indeed, this land has the particularity of being a small British overseas territory (6.8 km²) that shares a border of barely one kilometer with its Spanish neighbor. A piece of land that is no less strategic, since this territory gave its name to the famous Strait of Gibraltar, a maritime gateway between the Atlantic Ocean and the Mediterranean Sea.

Why a British territory so far from its metropolis? To understand this, it is necessary to look back into history. Until then a Spanish territory, Gibraltar came under the British flag in 1713 following the War of the Spanish Succession and the Treaty of Utrecht. Since then, this "rock" has not ceased to be claimed by Spain, especially in the 1960s. With the period of decolonization, the Spanish government tried to recover it by raising the issue before the United Nations, under the pretext of putting an end to the "colonial" situation of Gibraltar, according to the principle of "the right of peoples to self-determination". Faced with this diplomatic offensive, the United Kingdom counterattacked and submitted a referendum to the Gibraltarians in 1967. The result was clear: 99.64% of them expressed their desire to remain under British sovereignty. As a result, the dictator Franco, the Spanish leader at the time, closed the border between Spain and Gibraltar. This was not re-established until 1985.

The main point of disagreement concerns the control of territorial waters and fishing zones, since *de facto* the British crown has the advantageous situation of Gibraltar. This is why Spain wants the abrogation of the agreements dating from the eighteenth century. The context tends to evolve, since Madrid no longer seeks to recover the territory, but rather to establish a Spanish-British co-sovereignty (similar to what is done for Andorra with France). In 2016, Spain reformulated its proposal to share sovereignty, but the Gibraltarians, who had already rejected the idea in a referendum in November 2002, maintained their position. The relative autonomy of this British territory is regularly questioned by its imposing neighbor. For this reason, Gibraltar has been seeking ways to emphasize its special status vis-à-vis the European Union and the United Kingdom for several years.

One of these means is sport, and not just any sport, as the most popular sport among the 30,000 inhabitants of Gibraltar is soccer. Its history is ancient, since the game was introduced to Gibraltar by the British military in the 19th century and the first club, Prince of Wales FC, was created in 1892. Soccer developed afterwards with the appearance of many teams, leading to the establishment of a league. The national team of Gibraltar was formed in 1923, during a match against the team of Seville. However, this team only played against local clubs and not national teams. It was not until the 1993 Island Games that Gibraltar played its first international match against the (also British) island of Jersey.

While the 1990s saw the appearance of new "small" national teams, such as San Marino, in the qualifiers for the World Cup or the Euro, Gibraltar applied for membership of UEFA in 1999. The move was far from far-fetched, as teams such as the Faroe Islands, an autonomous territory of the Kingdom of Denmark, are members of this institution and play official international matches with their national team. However, the Faroese case is different because Denmark was not opposed to this request. But in the case of Gibraltar, although the United Kingdom agrees to see its territory play under its own colors, it is seen as an affront by Spain, which still hopes to recover this piece of land. Moreover, the Spanish territory is subject to strong regionalist demands, and Madrid is wary of a precedent that could inspire the Basque Country or Catalonia, which have already set up unofficial national teams.

After being refused numerous times, Gibraltar reapplied in 2007, this time with the support of three major associations (England, Scotland and Wales). Spain did not say its last word, however, and lobbied UEFA to restrict membership rules for soccer associations to sovereign states recognized by the United Nations. This is not the case for Gibraltar, a British overseas territory. The change in rules was contested on the Gibraltar side and the case was brought before the Court of Arbitration for Sport (CAS). Finally, in 2011, CAS ruled that Gibraltar's membership could not be refused because the new UEFA rules were only established after the initial applications in 1999 and 2007. Subsequently, the Gibraltar Football Association was officially accepted as a full member of UEFA on May 24, 2013, with only the Spanish and Belarusian federations objecting[30]. Thus, for the time being, UEFA does not allow any matches between the national teams of Gibraltar and Spain. Gibraltar's first official international match was on November 19, 2013, against Slovakia.

Gibraltar continues to strive to exist through sport by becoming a member of FIFA in 2016. However, it had a slow start, as like many small teams, the Gibraltar team finished last in the various qualifying groups with no wins, in the qualifying rounds for the 2016 and 2020 Euros and the 2018 World Cup. However, the situation is changing, especially thanks to the League of Nations, the new UEFA competition that allows teams of "the same level" to compete and, why not? to get an unexpected ticket for participation in the Euro. The selection is progressing well thanks to this competition because it is on the occasion of the latter that Gibraltar won its first two games in official competition, against Armenia (1-0) and Liechtenstein (2-1). The victories against national teams used to international confrontations have put forward a whole territory.

Although the Gibraltar team is often defeated, the interest of the existence of this national team is elsewhere, especially given the Brexit. This national team legitimizes Gibraltar a little more, with the dissemination of its flag, or the image of its atypical stadium on

---

30. Montague James, "Gibraltar moves closer to soccer independence," *New York Times*, May 2013.

the side of the rock, the Victoria Stadium. Important elements for this territory of the United Kingdom whose future is uncertain. In the Brexit referendum in 2016, nearly 95.6% of Gibraltarians voted for the United Kingdom to remain a member of the European Union. It must be said that every day, nearly 14,000 people cross the border from the Campo de Gibraltar, a neighboring Spanish territory where unemployment is close to 40%. With the Brexit, it is the entire economy of the Rock that is in danger. Faced with this risk, the head of the Gibraltar government, Fabian Picardo, wants to join the Schengen area, of which the United Kingdom is not a part, to preserve this freedom of movement. Gibraltar wants to follow the example of other micro-states in Europe, such as Liechtenstein, an associate member of this area. Spain and the United Kingdom have already held discussions in 2018 on the situation of Gibraltar, signing bilateral agreements on citizens' rights and on administrative, police and customs cooperation.

On January 31, 2020, the U.K. and Gibraltar did leave the European Union. However, the British and Spanish governments agreed in December 2020 on a principle that the U.K. and the EU could negotiate the terms of Gibraltar's participation in certain aspects of the Schengen agreement. Spain, however, remains on the lookout to reiterate its plan for co-sovereignty and grant dual passports to Gibraltarians, who would then regain freedom of movement. This would also allow Madrid to win a diplomatic battle that has been going on for several centuries. However, it will be difficult to question the existence of this territory, as its national soccer team is now a true ambassador of this small and strategic territory.

11.
ARMENIA-AZERBAIJAN

The conflict in Nagorno-Karabakh in recent months has brought to light the existing tensions between Armenia and Azerbaijan. While the virtues of sport are often put forward to ease diplomatic relations between two countries, the situation between the Armenian and Azeri states is such that no international meeting is now possible between their two national soccer teams. This situation is explained by the geopolitical situation of Nagorno-Karabakh, a region that both sides claim because of its historical past. No referee is ready to blow the whistle in this war game between two irreconcilable countries.

To conclude this list of "impossible matches", according to UEFA rules, it is appropriate to focus on one last case: Armenia and Azerbaijan. A match between these two countries can be questioned at first sight because these countries are not clearly defined as being part of Europe. They are in fact part of Western Asia and the Caucasus region, although the latter has had a history intimately linked to the European and Asian continents. Both states are, for example, members of the Council of Europe, an intergovernmental organization for the defense of human rights and the development of democratic stability in Europe. The soccer federations of both countries joined UEFA (in 1993 and 1994), not the Asian Football Confederation, only a few years after their independence.

Armenia and Azerbaijan are indeed young countries, having gained their independence in the early 1990s from the Soviet Union. However, both countries have had a tumultuous history since the beginning of the 20th century. After the First World War and the dissolution of the Transcaucasian Federation, Azerbaijan and Armenia declared their independence on the same day, May 28, 1918. A war broke out very quickly afterwards, as the two entities claimed territories that they considered to be historically and ethnically theirs. They were finally annexed by the USSR, which put an end to the conflict, for a time. The Soviet leader Stalin unilaterally decided that the region of Nagorno-Karabakh, populated mostly by Christian Armenians, should be returned to Azerbaijan, which had a Muslim majority. It was only when the Soviet empire disintegrated at the end of the 1980s that the nationalist tendencies of the two countries resurfaced, particularly in the Nagorno-Karabakh region.

In 1988, the local population revolted and the region declared itself a republic in its own right. This announcement leads to a series of violence in the territory, which quickly turns into war. The conflict continued after the dissolution of the USSR in 1991. While Armenia and Azerbaijan declared their independence, Nagorno-Karabakh did the same in order not to be attached to Azeri territory. This decision resulted in the establishment of a blockade by the Azeri government on the region and its main Armenian ally. After hundreds of deaths and injuries, the conflict was finally frozen in 1994, thanks to a cease-fire. Negotiations for the final resolution of the conflict took place in the Minsk Group, co-chaired by France, Russia and the United States, without a lasting solution being found.

The issue of Nagorno-Karabakh is still far from being resolved. The region even relapsed into war in 2016, when Azerbaijan launched an offensive to reclaim the territory, triggering the Four Days War. Nagorno-Karabakh, meanwhile, amended its constitution by referendum in 2017, taking the name of the republic of Artsakh, in reference to the tenth province of the kingdom of Armenia, thus reaffirming its desire not to be under Azeri control. The war resurfaced on September 27, 2020, when the city of Stepanakert was targeted by bombing, triggering a cascade of diplomatic incidents and the mobilization of Armenian and Azerbaijani armed forces. The war ended on November 10, 2020, when a trilateral ceasefire agreement was signed between Azerbaijan, Armenia and Russia, forcing the Armenian state to relinquish all remaining occupied territories surrounding Nagorno-Karabakh. Azerbaijan also gained direct land access to its enclave of Nakhichevan, *via* a corridor through Armenia. This will further exacerbate the tensions between these two enemies.

This war has forced UEFA to continue its ban on international matches between the national soccer teams of these two countries. There has been one attempt in the past, during the Euro 2008 qualifiers. By chance, Armenia and Azerbaijan were placed in the same group. Unfortunately, the matches will never take place, as the two states did not reach a compromise. The matches were simply cancelled and both teams ended up in the last places of the group. This is proof that sport is far from being apolitical and that it cannot solve all the problems. Witness the recent history, when for example the Armenian player Henrikh Mkhitaryan refuses to go to the final of the Europa League 2019 because it takes place in Baku, the capital of Azerbaijan. The player and the Armenian Football Federation also react in September 2020, the period of the conflict in Nagorno-Karabakh, when a leader of the Azeri club Qarabağ FK is accused of publishing a message of hatred towards Armenia and defending the Armenian genocide of 1915. Despite calls for the exclusion of the club from European competitions, nothing is acted upon.

Indeed, Qarabağ FK is a characteristic example of Armenia-Azerbaijan tensions. The club was founded in 1951 in the town of Agdam, located in Nagorno-Karabakh. The town was taken over in 1993 by the armed forces of the new regional republic, leading to the exodus of its Azeri inhabitants and the club's move to the capital, Baku. Yet since its takeover in 2001 by one of Azerbaijan's largest companies, Azersun Holding, Qarabağ FK has established itself as the country's leading club. This is far from insignificant since, unlike Armenian clubs, Qarabağ FK is starting to become a regular in European competitions. In fact, it was the first Azeri club to qualify for the group stage of the Champions League in 2017. Thanks to this exposure, Azerbaijan is thus better placed on a map by millions of viewers. This sporting success bears the seal of the team's coach, Gurban Gurbanov, who wants to make it a sporting reference, "the Barcelona of the Caucasus", and the showcase of the Azeri cause demanding their return to Nagorno-Karabakh. Soccer is also a relay for the supporters of the independence of the "Republic of Artsakh". The region's national team has participated in several unofficial international matches since 2012, even hosting a 2019 CONIFA European Cup in Nagorno-Karabakh, which we will discuss in more detail in a few chapters.

On the Azeri side, soccer is not just a sport. Azerbaijan has been investing in recent years to become a new sporting stronghold. European Games in 2015, Formula 1 Grand Prix since 2016, Europa League final 2019 and, this summer, Euro 2021 matches in Baku. Azerbaijan has followed the lead of many other countries that use the organization of sporting events to attract international attention and improve the image of this country with an authoritarian regime. According to the country's Minister of Sports, Azad Rahimov, for whom "[each] of these events strengthens the place of Azerbaijan on the world map and creates conditions for increasing tourism"[31], and who boasts the "83 million viewers who watched the Baku Formula 1 Grand Prix in 2018. If the Euro 2021 matches do take place in Baku, they will also highlight a country that has been investing in soccer for many years. As evidenced by Socar, the national oil company, a major sponsor of UEFA since 2013, which bought the sponsorship of Atletico de Madrid at a high price so that the country's tourism slogan (*Land of fire*) would be displayed on the club's shirt from 2013 to 2015.

However, the desire to exist thanks to sport through major international events can have a downside, because if Azerbaijan is in the spotlight, so is its political regime. The conflict in Nagorno-Karabakh is becoming increasingly internationalized, as this strategic territory is of interest to many neighboring powers, including Russia, Iran and Turkey. Moreover, the Turkish state is Azerbaijan's main ally, providing logistical, humanitarian and military support. This support reflects the strong cultural and linguistic ties between the two countries, often referred to by the slogan "One Nation, Two States. Armenia, for its part, warns Turkey against a possible expansionist project, although the Armenian state is considerably weakened following the defeat in the Nagorno-Karabakh war. It is likely that this issue will come back to the forefront with the possible holding of the games in Baku.

---

31. AFP Dispatch, "Europa League: in Baku, sport as a showcase for the regime," May 2019.

IV. Atypical teams and competitions

12.
THE OTHER EUROPE OF SOCCER: CONIFA

While the Euro soccer tournament is taking place this summer, another competition should have been back on the field: the European Cup of the Confederation of Independent Football Associations (CONIFA). This tournament has finally been postponed because of the Covid-19 pandemic. This is bad news for an organization that has the particularity of highlighting soccer teams representing certain minorities, ethnic groups and contested regions, but which exist thanks to soccer.

While the greatest soccer nations will play the 16th edition of the Euro, another European Cup should have taken place at the same time, finally postponed because of the Covid-19 pandemic. That of the Confederation of Independent Football Associations (CONIFA), an organization that brings together teams from states not recognized at the international level, such as those from minorities and disputed regions. These teams are not eligible to join the official world soccer organization, FIFA, because of a lack of infrastructure and because such "national teams" cause diplomatic difficulties with certain states. This is the challenge of CONIFA, which wants to highlight populations with complex geopolitical situations. This confederation was born on June 7, 2013, after the disappearance of the NF-Board, which had been organizing competitions between such teams since 2006. According to its statutes, its objective is "to contribute to the strengthening of global relations and to build bridges between people, nations, minorities and isolated regions around the world through friendship, culture and the joy of playing soccer"[32].

This organization takes up the torch in a good way, since it organizes several international competitions, the first of which was a World Cup that took place in 2014 in Lapland (we will come back to this in more detail in the next chapter). Many teams are then present, such as the Kurdistan - the Kurds forming a population without a real state, living mainly in Turkey, Iran, Iraq and Syria -, or Abkhazia, a territory that proclaimed its independence from Georgia in 1992 but whose situation is recognized for the time being only by a few states, including Russia. Among the 12 teams involved, the County of Nice, a selection of players set up to promote the culture and identity of Nice, won the trophy against the Isle of Man. For Franck Delerue, player of the County of Nice, "it was an incredible experience, we changed countries, we discovered new cultures, regions of the world that we did not know at all"[33].

Since then, two other editions of this World Cup have been held. In 2016 in Abkhazia and in 2018 in London, where the host team was Barawa, a Somali diaspora based in the UK. It was in fact on this occasion that the CONIFA competition brought together the most teams, 16, from Tibet to the Tuvalu Islands via Kabylia. Nearly 3,000

---

32. CONIFA's website.
33. MENETIER Denis, " Comté de Nice, Ruthénie subcarpatique, Abkhazie... bienvenue à la CONIFA, l'antichambre de la FIFA ", *France TV Sport*, February 2021.

spectators from all walks of life gathered in the Enfield stadium. The strong Cypriot community in the British capital mobilized to support the finalist team, the Turkish Republic of Northern Cyprus, which, as its name indicates, is a territory in the northeast of the island of Cyprus, recognized only by Turkey. In the end, the team from Subcarpathian Ruthenia (to which I will return later) won this edition. However, the organization of such competitions is not easy because, unlike the influential FIFA, only the players' stay is insured. This implies that the travel expenses, the staff and the rest are taken care of by the team. This complicates the travel of selections from America, Asia or Africa, the CONIFA tournaments being organized mainly in Europe, and forces many to give up participating due to lack of funds.

In addition to the material constraints, other problems come into play. Notably the diplomatic dimension since some countries do not want their territorial integrity to be challenged, like China, which protested against the presence of the Tibetan team at the 2018 CONIFA World Cup, or Ukraine, in reaction to the victory of Subcarpathian Ruthenia, a region of Ukraine with a large Hungarian minority, at the same World Cup. The Ukrainian authorities then denounced a "sports separatism", which resulted in a ban on the selected players to play at professional and amateur level in Ukraine.

Other selections have different claims, such as Cascadia. This team represents the bio-region of the same name, in the northwest of the American continent. At the same World Cup, when reporter Matthew Engel asks the question, "Who is oppressing the Cascadians?" a player on the team replies, "Anyone who harms the planet."[34]

---

34. DUEZ Julien, "We were at the CONIFA World Cup final," *So Foot*, June 2018.

Diplomatic problems remain the main obstacle to the development of these selections, as shown by the example of the last European Cup CONIFA 2019 in a highly sensitive region, Nagorno-Karabakh or Artsakh Republic. This competition is indeed a way for the region to highlight its status as a self-proclaimed republic, vis-à-vis Azerbaijan, which claims sovereignty over this territory. This has led to pressure from the Azeri side for some teams not to participate - this is the case for the teams from Sardinia and the Donetsk People's Republic. However, the European Cup did take place and South Ossetia won the final against Western Armenia.

However, Per-Anders Blind, president of CONIFA, denies any politicization of the events: "We don't do politics. Soccer is in my blood and I don't care about politics. Our members are often people who have been historically brutalized and who have low self-esteem. CONIFA's goal is simply to give them the opportunity to show their beauty, and to educate the world about them.[35] Brutalized populations in the image of the Chagos Islands, which represents a people of the Indian Ocean expelled from their islands more than 50 years ago by the United Kingdom to make a U.S. military base on the main island of Diego Garcia.

The 2020 World Cup was supposed to be held in a less sensitive area, in northern Macedonia, but like many events, it was postponed because of the Covid-19 pandemic. However, CONIFA and its 60 member federations did not give up and, at its general assembly in January 2021, confirmed that a new European Cup would be held until the situation was clarified. Finally, the announcement fell on May 5, 2021: this competition is finally postponed.

---

35. MENETIER Denis, "Comté de Nice, Ruthénie subcarpatique, Abkhazie... bienvenue à la CONIFA, l'antichambre de la FIFA", *France TV Sport*, February 2021.

CONIFA European President Alberto Rischio said, "We hope that this great and popular tournament can be held in Nice next year and we look forward to seeing you in 2022."[36] There is also doubt that the first ever CONIFA Women's World Cup will be held this summer in Sicily, a former Transylvanian region with large Hungarian and Romanian minorities.

The two competitions are intended to bring together a number of selections with different claims, such as the regionalism of the British county of Cornwall or greater international recognition for South Ossetia. For example, they will allow the Sicilian country, the host federation of the Women's World Cup, to highlight the history of its people. For Kristof Wenczel, vice-president of CONIFA, "this is a huge leap forward for the organization, and an important step in the history of the Sicilian country"[37].

Despite CONIFA's good intentions, the organization is beginning to experience the same problems as its big sister, FIFA, related to power issues. Paul Watson, former organizer of the 2018 CONIFA World Cup, points to the fact that some European federations are favoured over others, especially in view of their economic base. In other words, if the federations, most of which are volunteers, do not pay their dues, they cannot participate in CONIFA competitions.

Be careful that this beautiful project of highlighting peoples or minorities often ignored does not turn into a place where favoritism reigns. And that the competitions of this summer allow to put forward the fights of many contested regions. In any case, the "resistance" is getting organized, as some CONIFA members have formed the World Unity Football Alliance, a group of federations seeking to organize competitions for themselves, without any hierarchy or

---

36. CONIFA website, press release of May 5, 2021.
37. CONIFA website, press release of January 31, 2021.

political games. The Jersey team, meanwhile, is seeking to organize a tournament with teams recognized by FIFA and UEFA so that new bridges can be built through soccer.

In any case, these different selections demonstrate once again that soccer is not only a simple sport and allows to express oneself as much by the feet as by the words.

13.
LAPLAND:
THE NATIONAL SELECTION OF SANTA'S LAND

Proof of the global impact of soccer, even Santa Claus has taken up the cause! Beyond this narrative facility, Lapland is indeed a territory composed of an ancient indigenous people, the Sami. Soccer remains today one of the rare elements of unity of this people that spreads over four different countries.

Lapland. This name is not insignificant since it is often associated with the imaginary country of Santa Claus, populated by reindeers and elves. However, this territory is very real. It extends in the northern regions of four countries, namely Norway, Sweden, Finland and northwest Russia. Throughout its history, Lapland has been inhabited by the indigenous nomadic Sámi people, who today number 100,000. This people should not be called "Lappish", because this term has a pejorative character in Swedish: it means "ragged". This is why the territory is not called Lapland in the local language, but Sápmi.

The term "discriminatory" is not surprising if one refers to history, since this minority was the object of persecution throughout the

20th century. The various Sami peoples established in Norway and Sweden tried to unite as early as 1917 with the first Sami congress in 1917 in Trondheim, Norway. This was the first time that Norwegian and Swedish Sami people met outside their national borders to work together to find solutions to common problems. These different populations were finally assimilated. This was the case in Norway, where a policy was put in place with the aim of "absorbing these people" and integrating them into the Norwegian nation, *via* laws restricting the right of the Sami to buy land, practice their culture or even speak the Sami language, until 1959. The same is true in Sweden, where discrimination continued until 1970.

The situation for the locals improved afterwards, as the rights of this people were gradually recognized. The Sámi establish means to promote their culture. They use for it in particular the sport and the round ball. On July 19, 1985, a team from the Great North played its first international match against Åland, an autonomous province of Finland. Lapland finally lost with a score of 4 goals to 2, but the interest was elsewhere. This match is above all historical. It was broadcast live on the radio in northern Norway and Sweden, highlighting this people who had been forgotten and persecuted for too long. The players of the time still remember it, as Kalle Tjäder, the very first striker of the Lapland team, testifies: "It was wonderful. It was Lapland's first international match and we had to score. I really didn't expect it.[38]

This match was part of the Sámi social movement of the 1980s for greater recognition of their rights as an indigenous people. Progress led to the Nordic Sami Conference in Åre, Sweden, on August 15, 1986, which adopted the first Sami flag, with red, green, yellow and blue colors, decorated with a circle representing the sun and the

38. Kejonen Olle, "1985: Sápmis första landskamp," *Sverige Radio*, August 2015.

moon. Subsequently, the Norwegian, Swedish and Finnish "Sami Parliaments" were created to bring the claims of this minority to the attention of national governments. This is not the case on the Russian side, where no such representative body is recognized. The three parliaments often work together on cross-border issues, but there is no single unified Sami parliament covering the Nordic countries. At present, they have very little political influence, far from autonomy.

The Lapland team continued its rise with matches against real national teams such as the East German hopefuls in 1987, or Estonia in 1990. A rapid development that pushed the Lapland Football Association to apply for membership in FIFA in 2001, imitating the Danish territory of the Faroe Islands. The procedure was not successful and the Lapland team continued its world tour. Since 2000, federations have been created to allow teams that are not accepted as members of FIFA to compete.

The Nordics hit a great blow in 2006, by winning the Viva World Cup 2006, one of the first international competitions of this type for these selections[39]. The final victory is without appeal, 21-1, against the national team of Monaco! This is partly due to the fact that the Sámi national team had several professional players in the Norwegian and Swedish leagues, including former Norwegian international Tom Høgli, who later became a true ambassador of the Sámi identity.

This performance allows the Lapland team to put forward its culture and its fight for more recognition. Above all, this selection brings together on paper all the Sami communities, while on the political field the parliaments are not yet united. Because of this lack of unity, the question of autonomy for the region is not yet

---

39. DOWLING Tim, "The World Cup sides you've never heard of", *The Guardian*, June 2008.

13. Lapland: the national selection of Santa's land

on the agenda. The struggle of this selection is more focused on a better consideration of the rights of the indigenous population. This lack of coordination does not help the Lapland team to develop and prevents it from fulfilling the requirements for membership in the soccer organizations of FIFA or UEFA. As a result, the team is still unable to participate in official international matches or tournaments, such as the World Cup qualifiers. However, the team's various tours have played a major role in raising international awareness of the rights of the Sami people.

This momentum slowed down in the early 2010s, as the Lapland Football Association experienced significant financial problems, which led to the creation of a new structure in 2014, the FA Sápmi. The latter wasted no time in hosting the first ever CONIFA World Cup in 2014 in the Swedish city of Östersund. It brings together 12 teams, ranging from Kurdistan to the Isle of Man via Nagorno-Karabakh. The team from Lapland did not win any match and let the County of Nice win the competition.

The Sámi subsequently participate in other international tournaments, another World Cup in 2016 in Abkhazia and the 2019 European Cup in Nagorno-Karabakh. Lapland failed to win these competitions. It is currently ranked 15th in the CONIFA world rankings, and the team has not won an international title since its 2006 trophy. They are no longer the top team in the non-FIFA world. Part of the reason for the team's lackluster performance is the increasing reluctance of professional clubs in Norway and Sweden to release their same-origin players due to an increasingly busy schedule. The interest is elsewhere for this team. Above all, it is a way of highlighting the identity of the Sami nation, of which 85,000 people claim to be Sami, through a collective and cross-border project, and of making Lapland and its history more visible to the world.

14.

San Marino: the "smallest" soccer team in Europe

San Marino, one of the smallest and oldest states in the world, uses its soccer team as a true ambassador to exist on the international scene. Beyond the numerous defeats of this selection, the football is above all a diplomatic means for this tiny country to promote its independence, acquired more than 1,700 years ago.

Let's go to the Italian boot, where one of the smallest states on our planet is located: San Marino, a territory of about 60 km² and 34,000 inhabitants, landlocked in the middle of Italy. It is the third smallest country in Europe, after the Vatican City and Monaco, and the fifth smallest country in the world. This territory is indeed tiny, but its history is rich. San Marino is probably the oldest republic in the world. Which, as we shall see, explains why this small country is so keen to have its soccer team promote the country.

For San Marino, everything begins in the year 257. According to the legend, the stonemason Marinus participated in the reconstruction of the walls of the city of Rimini, after their destruction by Liburnian pirates. He could not finish his work because he was forced to flee the city, following a wave of persecution launched against the Christians by the Roman emperor Diocletian. Marinus built himself a refuge in the heights of Mount Titano, which later became a monastery where he lived as a hermit. As the persecution continued, Christians came to take refuge under the protection of this saint Marinus. And it is on September 3, 301 that the date of birth of San Marino is conventionally fixed.

Over time, this small territory faced various assaults and managed to preserve a certain independence on its heights. It became a city-republic, with its own legal code, and then a constitution from the year 1600. San Marino thus claims to be the oldest existing sovereign state and constitutional republic. A particularism that the San Marinese have defended tooth and nail over the centuries despite invasions, thanks to a skilful sense of diplomacy. Already, during the Napoleonic wars, the republic was recognized by Napoleon through the treaty of Tolentino, in 1797. Then during the Italian wars of independence, San Marino took in one of the "fathers of the Italian fatherland", Giuseppe Garibaldi, thus avoiding being integrated into modern Italy in 1861. To ensure its back, the small republic even wrote to the president of the United States at the time, Abraham Lincoln, and offered him an alliance. This clever maneuver allowed San Marino's independence to be confirmed after the signing of a treaty of friendship with Italy in 1862. Since then, despite the troubles and wars in Europe, San Marino has managed to preserve its independence and its republic. For the record, it is one of the only countries where a communist government was democratically elected to power, from 1945 to 1957.

However, full autonomy is not everything. To continue to exist at the international level, the country developed key sectors such as tourism, wine and stamps, and joined various international bodies.

The small country became a state recognized by its peers, joining the Council of Europe in 1988 and the United Nations in 1992. The republic goes even further by intensifying its sports diplomacy to make its flag live in the world. Already present at the Olympic Games since 1960, it joined UEFA and FIFA in 1988.

Soccer is one of the most popular sports in San Marino, along with basketball and volleyball. The San Marino Football Federation was created in 1931, followed very quickly by a first competition in 1936, the Coppa Titano. It was only much later, in 1985, that soccer was really organized with the first official San Marino championship, with 15 teams. The national team, the *Serenissima, was* born a year later, in 1986, and played its first international match, unofficially, against the Canadian Olympic team, with a defeat by 1 to 0. A disappointment which will call for others after its membership in various soccer organizations. Out of nearly 174 games played, the San Marino team has almost only lost. The most notable being a bitter 13-0 defeat against Germany during the Euro 2008 qualifiers.

However, there is a golden age for the San Marino national team: the 1993 World Cup qualifiers. After a historic draw against Turkey, the team faced England in the final round. This game is important for the English, because a victory with a large goal difference can qualify them for the World Cup in the United States. However, after 8'3" of play, San Marino opened the score. Davide Gualtieri enters the history of the World Cup by scoring the fastest goal of the qualifiers. A trivial goal, since the English finally win 7-1, but the important thing is that the goal makes the headlines around the world. As Gualtieri recalls, "the coach had told us to play the first ball right away, to attack, because we would have very few opportunities during the game. The way the action developed left no room for doubt. This goal is not just a stroke of luck"[40]. This feat goes beyond borders. The 1995 match when San Marino travelled to Scotland was a case in point, with the Scottish fans coming to the stadium wearing shirts with the words "Gualtieri - eight seconds" on them.

Despite this achievement, San Marino will need a bit of luck to win their first match in official competition. So far, the team has won only one match out of more than 170 games, in a friendly against Liechtenstein on 28 April 2004. Andy Selva, the best scorer in the history of the *Serenissima*, who scored the winning free kick, remembers: "The best goal was the one against Liechtenstein in 2004, which led to a victory, the only one to date in the history of the team.[41] This success is not repeated in official competition. This means that the San Marino team, which has conceded almost 730 goals in its history against 24 scored, is still chasing a first victory. After the success against Liechtenstein, it was not until November 15, 2014, ten years ago, that San Marino drew 0-0 at home against Estonia, thus ending a sequence of 61 defeats.

This catastrophic record is explained by the fact that most of San Marino's players are not professionals, and have difficulty playing outside their home country. This is why Andy Selva, one of the few San Marino players to have played at a high level in Italy, has created the *Associazione Sammarinese Calciatori*, whose aim is to encourage the development of professionalism and to increase the resources of the soccer federation, which, for example, reimburses only 60 euros for the travel expenses of the amateur players of the selection. Moreover, for the time being, San Marino's soccer

40. CHADBAND Ian, "San Marino hero who humiliated England," *Evening Standard*, March 2003.
41. PAULUZZI Valentin, interview with Andy Sellva, *So Foot*, March 2015.

authorities are not naturalizing Italian footballers, despite requests from some of Italy's second and third division players.

Today, San Marino is the 210th national team in the FIFA world ranking, behind the British Virgin Islands and Anguilla. This places San Marino's national team in last place in world soccer. San Marino has even been overtaken in the ranking by the new kid on the block of European soccer, Gibraltar. Nevertheless, the soccer and Olympic sports events allow the oldest republic in the world to fly its flag and to exist internationally, even though this territory is only 60 km^2, the equivalent of the size of the city of Besançon.

As for other micro-states, San Marino must find ways to cultivate its reputation. Sport is one of its levers. Recently, soccer did it in the most beautiful way during the Euro 2020 qualifiers, where the only goal of the national team, after 9 defeats and 46 goals conceded, is the subject of many press articles. One fan even turned the goal into the famous song from the movie *Titanic*, "*My Heart Will Go On*", making this event one of the most shared San Marino sports feats on the Internet.

As for participation in a possible Euro soccer tournament, it seems utopian, although a new competition, the League of Nations, allows "small" teams to enter this major European tournament. San Marino does not have this objective for the moment, since its national team is the talk of the country "thanks" to its status of eternal loser. Sometimes it is better to be the red lantern to be highlighted, rather than being in the underbelly of the pack.

Second part:
BEYOND EUROPE

V. Soccer,
A Battleground Between Nations

15.
HONDURAS-SALVADOR:
THE SOCCER WAR

In 1969, Honduras and El Salvador, two neighboring countries in Central America, were engaged in a political dispute. At the same time, their two national soccer teams were competing for a spot in the 1970 World Cup. These simple soccer matches, however, ignite the flames that fan the flames of war between two "sister nations" whose respective governments have no choice but to exacerbate their hatred for each other.

"If there had been no football game in June 1969, another spark would surely have been found to ignite the hostilities."[42] This observation by José M. Delgado, rector of the University of San Salvador, sums up the heated context of the games between Honduras and El Salvador in June 1969. These matches took place in a climate so poisonous that they were nicknamed "the soccer war".

---

42. GHEMMOUR Chérif, *Terrain Miné, quand la politique s'immisce dans le soccer*, Hugo Sport, 2013, p. 132.

However, soccer was only a pretext to trigger the terrible conflict that ensued between Honduras and El Salvador, two neighboring Central American countries that share the same culture, the same language and the same flag colors (blue and white). How could a soccer match, which is a great popular celebration, be the catalyst of an almost fratricidal conflict? To answer this question, we need to look at history. The two countries gained their independence on the same day, September 15, 1821, and it is from the 1960s that they take very different paths.

One of the issues that has been deteriorating relations between the two countries is the demographic issue. El Salvador, in the south, is one of the smallest countries in Central America and has a population of nearly 4 million inhabitants at the time, or 200 inhabitants per km^2. Honduras, on the other hand, has a population of 3 million inhabitants for an area of 120,000 km^2, or 25 inhabitants per km^2. The Salvadoran population is so large that many emigrate to Honduran lands; in 1969, about 300,000 Salvadorans (10% of the total population of Honduras at the time) were working in the fields of their neighbor. This massive exodus was due to a very unequal distribution of land in El Salvador as well as, as we will see later, in Honduras. At the time, El Salvador was controlled by an oligarchic regime, in the hands of "14 families"; 2% of the total population owned more than 60% of the land. The high level of immigration even made General Arrelano, who took power in Honduras following a coup in 1963, say, "The Salvadorans are colonizing Honduras!"

However, the problems faced by the Honduran state have a name other than the specter of the foreigner: the United Fruit Company. The sprawling American multinational was a key player in Central America at the time. Its monopoly on the transport, sale and production of exotic products means that the various countries are obliged to go through it, which gives it a considerable power of influence to make and break governments. In Honduras, the situation is such that the American firm controls almost everything, from the ports to the railroads and the banks. Its political and economic base allows it to change laws with bribes. This is where the expression "banana republic" comes from, coined by the American author O. Henry. He was referring to states whose economies are based exclusively on the production of exotic fruits and which, in order to survive, must meet the demands of multinationals. It is difficult to resist when one knows that, for example, the United Fruit Company granted in 1975 the sum of 1.25 million dollars to the Honduran leader, General Arrelano, and a promise of another 1.25 million, in exchange for the reduction of taxes on banana exports.

This explains why in 1962 the agrarian reform, launched by the same Arrelano, was mainly to the advantage of the large landowners and served the interests of United Fruit. The weight of the multinational was very important, since in 1966 it managed to bring together many other large companies to create the National Federation of Honduran Farmers and Ranchers (FENAGH), thus sealing alliances with the richest farmers in Honduras. Thus, the reform measures do not address the heart of the problem of balancing the distribution of land. The Salvadoran immigrants, also forced by their political power to emigrate because of the lack of available land, were clearly held responsible and were gradually expelled from Honduras. The vacant land is given partially to small farmers, who are still not financially able to get by and blame the Salvadorans for all their ills.

15. Honduras-Salvador: the soccer war

El Salvador, for its part, does not want the return of its expelled nationals, because it would mean giving them land, thus amputating, once again, the large Salvadoran owners. Rather than finding a solution for a better distribution of wealth, the two governments are accusing each other. The territorial tension between the two neighbors had only just begun. The two authoritarian regimes set up a campaign of instrumentalization, the objective of which was to blame the national and agrarian problems on the neighbouring state, and thus to retain power, while reinforcing the advantages granted to the United Fruit Company. It was against this backdrop of heightened nationalist sentiment that El Salvador and Honduras met on a soccer field in June 1969.

The match is important because the winner will be one step closer to a historic qualification for the World Cup that will be held the following year in Mexico. The first match, on June 8, 1969, was played at home for Honduras, in Tegucigalpa. The latter won 1-0 against a tired El Salvador team. It must be said that the Salvadoran players had to face many problems in the Honduran capital. After slashing the tires of their bus, the opposing fans prevented them from sleeping all night. Ryszard Kapuściński, a journalist at the time and author of the book *The Football War and Other Wars and Adventures*, says: "The hotel was besieged by the crowd. The fans were whistling, shouting, screaming insults. This went on all night. All this was done with the aim of making their exhausted and exasperated hosts lose the match."[43] At the same time, new expulsions of Salvadoran farmers were carried out by the Honduran authorities.

On the soccer field, nothing is played yet. Honduras had to play one more match to qualify. But on June 15, 1969, it was El

---

43. Kapuściński Ryszard, *The Soccer War,* Granta Books, 1990.

Salvador, at home, that defeated its neighbor with a score of 3 goals to 0. Again, the conditions of the match were deplorable, the Honduran players having to change hotels the night before, the first one being burned. During these two matches, many exactions were committed in a camp as in the other one, and many were the injured, killed, raped supporters... Worse, after the first match, a young Salvadoran supporter, Amelia Bolanos, shot herself in the heart, desperate to see her team lose. A national funeral was held, and the Salvadoran government did not fail to point the finger of responsibility at Honduras.

In this poisonous climate, soccer takes a back seat. Each match is an opportunity for each regime to stir up hatred for the neighboring country. A final match must be played because, although El Salvador has scored more goals in both games, the *goal-average is not taken into* account. This means that a third match must be played to decide between the two teams. It took place on June 26, 1969.

Given the explosive situation, El Salvador broke off diplomatic relations with Honduras the day before. The match was relocated to a neutral ground in Mexico City. The match was played in a very tense atmosphere, as the supporters of both sides made it a matter of life and death. The players were no longer seen as sportsmen, but as soldiers armed with spikes who had to avenge humiliations. With Honduras leading 2-1, El Salvador finally won in extra time with a score of 3 goals to 2. Although the Salvadoran players are propelled to the rank of heroes, the sporting exploit is quickly eclipsed to make this victory an instrument at the service of the two authoritarian powers.

After the match, the governments of both countries continued to fan the nationalist flames, which contributed to an increase in border incidents. On Monday, July 14, 1969, the inevitable happened. A Salvadoran plane dropped a bomb in the Honduran capital, Tegucigalpa. The war, the real one, began. It is called the "Hundred Hours War". A short, almost fratricidal conflict, stopped under pressure from the international community, but above all by the lack of arms and fuel in two bloodless countries. Nevertheless, in one hundred hours, this war had the time to kill between 3,000 and 6,000 people and wound more than 15,000.

Thus, this El Salvador-Honduras is infamously dubbed the "soccer war," following the eponymous book by Ryszard Kapuściński that described these facts. The round ball played only a part in this diplomatic escalation. For the French anthropologist André-Marcel d'Ans, "[the] journalistic denomination of 'soccer war' gives the impression that these are peoples ready to fight over a simple ball story. It is very devaluing, this extremely violent war has nevertheless undermined the potential of each country for a very long time"[44].

After this deadly conflict, the Salvadoran people had nothing to celebrate after El Salvador's historic participation in the 1970 World Cup - they had qualified after a final match against Haiti. The "Salvadoran heroes" did not perform miracles in Mexico, they lost all three games against the host country, the USSR and Belgium, and did not score a single goal.

On the diplomatic front, the authoritarian regimes remained in place, still riding the xenophobic wave, and only signed a peace treaty in 1980. In addition to the fact that this war conside-rably strained relations between the two countries, it also halted the implementation of the Central American Common Market for 22 years, an economic union between Costa Rica, Guatemala,

---

44. GHEMMOUR Chérif, *Terrain Miné, quand la politique s'immisce dans le soccer, op. cit*, p. 132.

Honduras, Nicaragua and El Salvador that did not please the interests of the United Fruit Company in the region.

Since then, Honduras and El Salvador have met many times on the soccer field, but political tensions persist, with each political regime passing the buck to the neighboring country, blaming it for its internal problems. It is as if history is repeating itself, yet again.

16.

WHEN HONG KONG'S SOCCER TEAM TOPPLES CHINA

While China is putting pressure on Hong Kong to become fully Chinese, there was a time when Hong Kongers resisted Chinese hegemony through sport. This happened on May 19, 1985, on a soccer field. The humiliation of China was such that it triggered (already) a diplomatic conflict.

The Chinese vice is tightening around Hong Kong to make this territory, long British, a Chinese land in its own right. It must be said that on May 28, 2020, the Parliament of the People's Republic of China voted a law on national security. A text that, according to the newspaper *Le Monde*, "puts an end to the democratic exception of Hong Kong and considerably limits, even annihilates, the civil and political liberties of any citizen who disagrees with the Chinese system"[45]. This explains the numerous protests by Hong Kongers, who have always emphasized that they have a special status within

---

45. DE CHANGY Florence, "À Hongkong, la loi de sécurité imposée par la Chine met brutalement à fin à une exception démocratique", *Le Monde*, July 2020.

China. The case of a soccer match is a revealing event in this regard. On May 19, 1985, a qualifying match for the 1986 soccer World Cup was played between the two teams.

In 1985, Hong Kong was not yet under Chinese control. Indeed, since the Treaty of Nanking in 1842, Hong Kong was a British colony. It was not until 1997 that the Hong Kong territory was returned to China. Nevertheless, by the end of the 1970s, China was already keen to recover the two important trading areas of Hong Kong, held by the United Kingdom, and Macao, under Portuguese control.

It must be said that from 1978 onwards, China emerged from the long reign of Mao Zedong and sought to open up to the world with a series of economic reforms led by the new General Secretary of the Party, Deng Xiaoping. This opening was initially limited to special economic zones (SEZ). Among the first zones to benefit from these investments was the city of Shenzhen, located at the gateway to Hong Kong. It is experiencing spectacular development. The Hong Kong territory, then an important economic center, became a strategic issue for the Chinese People's Republic. As for the United Kingdom, it is difficult to see how it can preserve this territory, whose food supply depends largely on China.

On 19 December 1984, an agreement was reached. The Sino-British joint declaration on the question of Hong Kong was signed. This treaty provides that the United Kingdom will hand over Hong Kong, Kowloon and the New Territories to China on July 1, 1997. It was also through this treaty that the principle of "one country, two systems" began to be established for the 1997 handover. In other words, "socialism" as practiced in China would not be extended to Hong Kong and the territory would enjoy a high degree of auto-nomy. Meanwhile, the Chinese state also sought to establish its international power in the field of sports. Its great comeback at the 1984 Olympic Games in Los Angeles enabled it to finish fourth among the nations, with 32 medals obtained.

After its return on the Olympic scene, China also wants to make its entry on the soccer field by participating in the World Cup. It was played at a hair's breadth for the 1982 edition, after a final match of support lost 2-1 against New Zealand. Finalist of the 1984 Asian Cup of Nations, China is the favorite to qualify for the 1986 World Cup in Mexico. Their qualifying group seemed affordable, although the disputed colonies of Hong Kong and Macau were present. China won the first games of its group without difficulty, beating Brunei and Macao, with 22 goals scored for 0 conceded.

However, to qualify, China had to play a final match against Hong Kong on May 19, 1985. The two teams had already met in the first leg of the competition and were unable to break the tie at Hong Kong's Government Stadium. Before the final match, both teams had the same number of points. A draw is enough for the Chinese giant to qualify. China is the favorite in this match because it has already beaten its opponent by 2-0 in a qualifying match for the Asian Cup six months earlier, and also several times in the qualifying stages for the 1982 World Cup. The Chinese Empire thus had its fate in its own hands. At the same time, the Sino-British treaty was already begin-ning to exacerbate tensions between the two territories.

On May 5, 1985, a fortnight before the match, the teams of Hong Kong Seiko and the Chinese province of Liaoning came to blows. The atmosphere became even more electrifying. The Hong Kong team came to the Workers' Stadium in Beijing in front of more than 80,000 Chinese supporters. However, it was Hong Kong's Cheung Chi Tak who scored the first goal with a splendid free kick from 30 meters. China was quick to respond as Li Hui equalised 11 minutes later. While a draw would qualify the Chinese, the Hong

Kongese Ku Kam Fai extinguishes their hopes at the hour of play. The Chinese team does not manage to get back to the score. On the field, the Hong Kong team is officially qualified for the next round. In the stadium, the crowd went wild, humiliated at having been beaten by the small British colony.

This was the beginning of the riots of May 15, 1985, the first protest scene caused by Chinese soccer. Debris was thrown into the stadium, hundreds of cars were burned and the Chinese national team bus was overturned. It took the intervention of the Chinese police to stop this uprising, one of the worst incidents of public unrest that China has seen since 1949. Tensions were so high that the Chinese team was confined for three days after the match. According to official sources, more than 120 people were arrested. The president of the Chinese Football Association, Li Fenglou, and the coach of the national team, Zeng Xuelin, were forced to resign. The riots went around the world. The *South China Morning Post* headlined, "Hong Kong victory sparks riots."[46]

The victorious Hong Kongers were given a hero's welcome. Some waved the Hong Kong flag of the time, while others displayed a banner with the slightly exaggerated words "Champions of Asia".

However, in the next round, the valiant Hongkongers fell to Japan, by 5 to 1 over the two games, which put an end to their hopes of playing a World Cup. This epic remains the best performance of the Hong Kong soccer team in World Cup qualification.

On the Chinese side, it is the cold shower. It was not until the 2002 World Cup in Japan and South Korea that the Chinese team participated in the first World Cup in its history. But China is slow to become a nation that counts in the most popular sport in the world.

---

46. WOOD Chris, "When Hong Kong beat China in a World Cup qualifier 32 years ago, and riots that followed," *South China Morning Post*, May 2017.

Even if for several years, Xi Jinping, the president of the People's Republic of China, has been putting the means to make the Chinese team and players become major players on the soccer planet, with the ambitious goal of winning a World Cup by 2050.

After the events of 1985, Hong Kong and China met again on the soccer field, especially during the 2018 World Cup qualifiers. Both matches ended in draws and neither team managed to qualify. In Hong Kong, the historic May 19 match is still celebrated, and on its anniversary in 2015, a commemorative match is even held to celebrate the 30th anniversary of the historic 1985 victory.

Today, the battle is being played out on an entirely different terrain, as China wants to bring Hong Kong fully under its authority, even if it means using the hard way by imposing a law on national security that considerably restricts the Hong Kong exception. The issue has even moved into international territory, with the European Union and the United States condemning this Chinese "offensive", which is seen by its critics as an attack on individual freedoms and the territory's autonomy. The vice is tightening, however, since at the beginning of 2021, Beijing strengthened its grip on Hong Kong, with a reform of the electoral system that further restricts the voice of opponents.

17.

ARGENTINA-ENGLAND: WHEN MARADONA AVENGES THE FALKLANDS WAR

The Falkland Islands have been claimed by Argentina and the United Kingdom for several centuries. This territorial issue is at the heart of a legendary match of the 1986 World Cup. With as main protagonist the recently deceased star of football, Diego Armando Maradona.

"It was like we beat a country, not just a soccer team. Although we said before the game that soccer had nothing to do with the Falklands War, we knew [that the English] had shot a lot of young Argentines like little birds. So this match was a revenge."[47] With these words, taken from his autobiography, *Yo Soy El Diego*[48], the legendary footballer Diego Armando Maradona describes the backstage of Argentina's victory against England on June 22, 1986. This soccer match was indeed much more than a simple match, given the tense

---

47. GHEMMOUR Chérif, *Terrain Miné, quand la politique s'immisce dans le soccer, op. cit.* p. 172.
48. MARADONA Diego Armando, *Yo Soy El Diego*, Planeta, 2001.

diplomatic context between the two countries. At the center of this conflict, the Falklands.

It is a small archipelago of about 3,500 inhabitants, located off the coast of Patagonia and Argentina. However, this territory of 12,000 km², the size of Qatar, is for the moment British. Throughout history, many countries have fought to conquer these islands, be it France, Spain or the United Kingdom. In 1816, Argentina became independent and took over the Spanish claims on the islands. Due to its strategic position, the United Kingdom did everything possible to reconquer the Falklands in 1833 and gradually established settlers there. Since then, Argentina still claims sovereignty over this territory which it calls the *Malvinas*, while the United Kingdom calls them the Falkland Islands.

This situation created a climate of tension between Argentina and the United Kingdom. Although the two countries began negotiations in 1965, after the implementation of the United Nations Declaration on the Granting of Independence to Colonial Countries and Peoples, the situation remained stalled. It took a different turn the following years, when Argentina was under military dictatorship. All means were used to hide the serious economic and political problems of the country. The government struggled to unify the country, which had been suffering from violent political and social unrest for more than 30 years, which led to the establishment of a military dictatorship by General Videla in 1976. This new authoritarian political regime did not allow Argentina to recover, although the political instrumentalization of the 1978 soccer World Cup on its soil sought to give the country a better image internationally.

In search of legitimacy in the eyes of the population (annual inflation was then 140%) and guided by expansionist desires, the military junta, now led by General Galtieri, launched the seductive project of "bicontinental Argentina", whose objective was to allow the country to extend as far as Antarctica and to become an indisputable regional power. This will strengthen national sentiment. The Falklands are the perfect starting point for this project of conquest, as they are a gateway to Antarctica and are already very symbolic in the Argentine imagination.

Thus, on April 2, 1982, Operation Rosario began: Argentine soldiers launched the offensive on the British archipelago. It was a risky gamble, but the Argentine political establishment was banking on the fact that the alliance between Argentina and the United States would protect the country from a possible rout. The Conservatives in power in London, led by their Prime Minister Margaret Thatcher, were caught off guard by this military attack, which contradicted their intelligence. The government was initially accused of negligence. The "Iron Lady" counterattacked and built her legend by reacting in less than a week with a military response. After only two months of confrontations, on June 14, after 649 Argentinean and 255 British deaths, the Argentinean armed forces were forced to sign the peace. In Argentina, this final defeat precipitated the end of the military dictatorship; the first democratic presidential election in 1983 brought Raúl Alfonsín to power. On the British side, Thatcher was strengthened by this victory, which she followed up with an electoral success.

Three years later, in 1986, the two democracies, still at loggerheads over diplomacy, were serious contenders for the World Cup in Mexico. Diego Armando Maradona, 26 years old, was at the top of his game and also had a solid *Albiceleste,* the Argentine national team, while his English counterpart had a number of renowned players in great shape, such as Gary Lineker and Bryan Robson. After a relatively quiet group stage, both teams impressed with their

17. Argentina-England: When Maradona avenges the Falklands War

mastery in the round of 16, against Uruguay (1-0) and Paraguay (3-0) respectively. On June 22, in Mexico City's stadium, the two nations met for the first time since the Falklands confrontation.

The confrontation brings back other painful memories to the Argentines. In the 1966 World Cup, held on British soil, the quarter-final between England and Argentina turned into a real battle. The expulsion of the Argentine captain Antonio Rattin set off the fire. The player contested the decision and took ten minutes to leave the field, taking care in the process to tear the British flag from the corner post. It is from this confused situation that the red card was born, which directly expels a player from the match. The match was no longer a sporting affair. After the 1-0 victory of England, against a background of refereeing complacency, the *British* coach, Alf Ramsey, prevented his players from exchanging their shirts.

This stormy historical context is spiced up by the sulphurous statements of the Argentine players before the 1986 match. Nery Pumpido, Argentina's goalkeeper, warned, "Beating the English will be a double satisfaction for what happened in the Falklands."[49] The *Sun* announces "the landing of 5,000 men"[50] in reference to the English fans who made the trip.

It is noon in Mexico City, the heat is stifling, English flags are burning in the stands that house 115,000 people. A legendary match can begin. The confrontation is warlike, rough. The instructions were clear on the British side: leave no space for the prodigy Maradona, and dissuade him from keeping the ball. The Argentine number 10 was not spared, and the first half, pleasant in spite of everything, ended with a scoreless draw. But, as soon as the second half started, in the 51st minute, the first shot was fired.

---

49. CARLIN John, "England vs Argentina - A history", *The Guardian*, May 2002.
50. *Ibid.*

When the ball was not cleared properly and the English goalkeeper Peter Shilton was not sure of his exit, Maradona jumped forward and touched the ball with his left hand to score. The referee, Mr. Bennaceur, guided by his assistant and yet impeccable throughout this stormy match, makes an obvious mistake: the goal is validated, the *Mano de Dios* ("hand of God") is born. Three minutes later, the *Pibe de Oro* scored another masterful goal, this time in accordance with the rules. 10 seconds, 50 meters, 6 players eliminated: Maradona scored the *Gol del Siglo* ("goal of the century"), to the delight of an Argentine commentator on the verge of orgasm, who described it live as a "cosmic kite. The Englishman Gary Lineker even said that he felt like clapping at an opponent's goal for the only time in his career.

He headed the ball home in the 81st minute, but the game was over: Argentina, thanks to a diabolically brilliant Maradona, eliminated England. The Argentine would later say: "We said we shouldn't mix soccer and politics, but that was a lie. I got my hands on the ball to take revenge on the English, who got their hands on the Falklands."

The Argentine star, who scored twice against the Belgians in the semi-final, led his team to the title, which they won against Germany 3-2, and was the best player of the tournament (5 goals, 5 assists).

Since then, several matches have reminded us of the rivalry between the two countries. In 1991, at Wembley, Maradona came out on the pitch ostensibly holding the ball with his left hand. In 2002, during a confrontation at the World Cup, the Argentinean anthem was loudly whistled by the English fans. Above all, during the 1998 World Cup in France, the players of both teams almost came to blows. The Englishman David Beckham loses his nerves in front of the boiling Diego Simeone, before, finally, the Argentinians win after a stormy penalty shoot-out.

17. Argentina-England: When Maradona avenges the Falklands War

If the last meeting between them dates back to 2005, the geopolitical conflict remains present. The strong commemoration of the thirtieth anniversary in 2012 in Argentina, the anti-British rhetoric of Cristina Kirchner (president of Argentina from 2007 to 2015) reactivate the tensions. Why so much virulence from both countries for such a small archipelago? The control of fishing zones is a factor, but it is above all the discovery, in 2010, of an oil field of 350 million barrels in relatively shallow waters, which rekindles tensions around the archipelago. Beyond the financial aspect, the Falklands form an interesting anchor point for the United Kingdom at a time when the South American continent is beginning to emerge; in addition, the archipelago has become a symbol of British resistance abroad, far from its bases. The inhabitants are in any case attached to the British Crown since they voted in a referendum in March 2013 for the territory to remain British, with nearly 99.8% of the vote.

Be that as it may, the Anglo-Argentine rivalry, on and off the field, has not ended. Although the two governments reached an agreement in 2016 to boost growth there, the Brexit is plunging this British overseas territory into uncertainty. This reopens the question of sovereignty over these islands. With the new political situation in Europe, Buenos Aires hopes to resume negotiations.

Argentina's Secretary of State for Falkland Islands Affairs, Daniel Filmus, said, "It is not possible that for 188 years a part of our country has been usurped by a colonial power."[51] Proof that the Falkland Islands/Malvinas issue will continue to spice up relations between Argentina and the United Kingdom for a long time to come.

---

51. Cavalonne Elena, "With Brexit, uncertainty looms over the future of the Falkland Islands," *Euronews,* January 2021.

18.

Qatar-Saudi Arabia: the new soccer duel?

The small Middle Eastern emirate has managed in a few decades to become a major player in world sport and to occupy the central place in soccer. To the point of acquiring the Paris-Saint-Germain club and obtaining the organization of the next World Cup 2022. With the objective of making Qatar grow through sport. A success that does not please his great regional rival, Saudi Arabia, which seeks for some years to imitate the Qatari strategy to benefit from the positive effects of this sports soft power.

In 2022, Qatar and its 11,000 km^2 will host one of the biggest international sporting events, the Football World Cup. This is quite an achievement, considering that previous editions have been hosted by much larger countries in terms of size: Russia in 2018, Brazil in 2014, and South Africa in 2010. Because, yes, Qatar is very small on the scale of the planet, with a size comparable to the region of Ile-de-France. This Middle Eastern nation has a population of barely 2.5 million, of which only 10% are nationals. This fragile demographic configuration is doubled by the presence of its great

133

neighbor and rival: Saudi Arabia and its 2,000,000 km^2, the 13th largest country in the world. However, it is the small Qatari territory that will host the World Cup next year. This is a coup for the Gulf state, which already owns the Paris-Saint-Germain football club and has a strong presence in the sports world, notably through its media group beIN Sports and its various sponsors. By being so present in the sports field, Qatar aims to exist in the eyes of the world.

Indeed, this country gained its independence less than 50 years ago, in 1971. Very quickly it had to find ways to extricate itself from the influence, and even interference, of its neighbors, in particular the Saudi power. It is from 1995, under the leadership of Emir Hamad ben Khalifa Al Thani, that Qatar detached itself from its tutelage to fully exist on the international scene. Well helped, it is true, by the income from the exploitation of its gas-rich subsoil to support its influence strategy. Qatar then undertook to gain power in the region. The Qatari government launched the Al Jazeera news channel in 1996 to break the Saudi monopoly in the Arab media. This strategy of influence is better known as *soft power*.

In order to consolidate this power, to seduce the international community and to preserve its territorial integrity in the face of its powerful neighbors, Qatar has been quick to rely on sport and its universal values. As Sheikh Ahmed Ben Abdallah Al-Sulaîti, CEO of Qatar National Broadband Network, reminds us in the newspaper *L'Équipe*, "Saudi Arabia is the country of oil, Bahrain the financial hub, Dubai the commercial hub. To exist on the international scene, Qatar had the choice of industry and sport. And sport is the ideal vector"[52]. Problem: the emirate was far from being a sporting nation in the 1990s, despite its affiliation to FIFA since 1970. However, the

52. GUÉGAN Jean-Baptiste, *Géopolitique du sport, une autre explication du monde*, Bréal, 2017, p. 165.

Gulf country invested heavily to become a central place in world sport. The first stone in the building of this future empire was the organization of an international tennis tournament in the capital, Doha, in 1993. This was soon followed by participation in equestrian, sailing, motor sports and golf competitions.

This ambitious diplomacy through sport has gradually moved on to more mainstream sports. The first of them is soccer. Qatar has entered the world of football through the front door, since on December 2, 2010, it is the consecration: the organization of the 2022 World Cup is awarded. This was a surprise as the Emirate is far from being a country with a footballing tradition! However, since the beginning of the 2000s, it has been working behind the scenes within the sport's governing bodies to gain influence. However, the surprise is such that the vote for this award is the subject of many suspicions of corruption within FIFA, as revealed in the book *The Man Who Bought a World Cup. The Qatari plot*[53], by journalists Heidi Black and Jonathan Calvert. The suspicions are confirmed through an FBI investigation and the Garcia report on the controversial awarding of the 2018 and 2022 World Cups, respectively to Russia and Qatar. The institution of FIFA is shaken by its affairs, which lead in particular to the resignation of its president, Sepp Blatter, as well as the arrest of several senior executives of the organization in 2015. However, the 2022 World Cup remains awarded to Qatar.

On the geopolitical ground, this Qatari consecration is terribly tending to relations in the Middle East. Especially with Saudi Arabia, which thus sees its small neighbor gain in global prestige. Relations between these two states have been deteriorating since the early 2010s, with the emergence of the Arab Spring, with both

---

53. BLAKE Heidi and CALVERT Jonathan, *The Ugly Game: The Qatari Plot to Buy the World Cup,* Simon&Chuster, 2016.

18. Qatar-Saudi Arabia: the new soccer duel?

countries supporting different sides. Diplomatic escalation culminated in a blockade of Qatar by Saudi Arabia and its allies in 2017, with Riyadh accusing its rival of supporting terrorist organizations and having close ties to the region's other major power, Iran. Despite the large force and threats of military attacks, Qatar has managed to keep its economy afloat and mobilize the international community around its case. Its political and sporting influence is not for nothing. Worse, the blockade weakens the already precarious economic balance of the region. Since then, relations have tended to warm up, even though Qatar's ever-increasing role in world sports bodies has irritated its large neighbor. The situation seems to be calming down, at least, since at the beginning of 2021, Saudi Arabia has lifted the blockade.

Qatar's *success story*, thanks to its sports diplomacy, is giving ideas to the Saudi petromonarchy. Indeed, Saudi Arabia has been seeking, since the early 2010s, to modernize and diversify its economy, which is ultra-dependent on fossil fuels (31% of its GDP and 79% of its export revenues in 2018). Problem: between the case of critical journalist Jamal Khashoggi, killed inside the Saudi consulate in Istanbul in 2017, and the controversial military intervention in Yemen since 2015, not to mention accusations of human rights abuses, Saudi Arabia's image has deteriorated considerably over the years. As for women's rights, although Saudi women now have the right to drive and have a national championship, they are almost non-existent since they remain legally under the guardianship of their "guardian", father, husband or son.

Faced with such a situation, what better way than sport to modernize the image of the monarchy and attract foreign investors to diversify its economy. While reinforcing its regional domination in the Persian Gulf, by not letting Qatar take too much control. It is therefore through sport that Saudi Arabia has chosen to restore its image. This sports *soft power* is part of a more global strategy, called Vision 2030. Launched in 2016, this plan is the brainchild of Crown Prince Mohammed bin Salmane, Minister of Defense at the time, who now holds the reins of the country. Vision 2030 wants to modernize the Saudi regime by increasing international partnerships, strengthening services to the population, modernizing institutions and investing in key sectors such as sustainable development, new technologies and tourism.

Qatar, however, is far ahead of the game. Already in the early 2000s, the Qatar Foundation logo appeared on the jersey of one of the most popular clubs in the world, FC Barcelona. Above all, on May 31, 2011, the Qatari state investment fund Qatar Sport Investment (QSI) bought the Paris-Saint-Germain club for 70 million euros[54]. This was a strategic choice, both to restore the colors of a historic club on the national and European scene, but also to associate Qatar with the most visited city in the world, Paris, and thus gain in visibility. In ten years, thanks to Qatari investments, PSG has become one of the biggest brands in soccer, with nearly 75 million fans worldwide. Qatar can also rely on the fame of international stars Neymar or Kylian Mbappé, recruited at a high price by the club of the capital (422 million euros between them). Knowing that the Gulf country can rely on its network of sports channels beIN Media Group, created in 2011, which, present in over 40 countries on five continents, is considered the largest buyer of sports rights in the world.

Long in the shadow of other oil states in the region, and their ambitious sports policies, the Saudi regime has shifted gears in 2019 to attract sports event organizers and fans from around the

____

54. GUÉGAN Jean-Baptiste, *Géopolitique du sport, op. cit,* p. 170.

world. Since the $100 million *Clash of Dunes* boxing match between stars Anthony Joshua and Andy Ruiz in 2019, the Saudi state has hosted the Saudi International Golf and more events are on the way, such as the first ever Saudi Arabian Grand Prix in 2021. It should be noted that neighboring Bahrain and the United Arab Emirates also have their own Formula 1 car races. In soccer, Saudi Arabia does not have a World Cup like its Qatari neighbor, but it is becoming a destination for other competitions, such as the Italian and Spanish Super Cups, which pit recognized European teams against each other.

Saudi Arabia has also succeeded in securing the Dakar Rally and the organization of a cycling tour on its territory in 2020. These competitions give it the opportunity to attract foreign advertisers, but also to showcase the country's landscapes, and thus make the Saudi territory known to a global audience. As Carole Gomez, director of research in geopolitics of sport at the IRIS Institute, explains, "the idea is to showcase the beauty of the landscape, the infrastructure that can accommodate you if you come on a trip, and to make a postcard of Saudi Arabia"[55]. Recall that since opening its borders to foreign tourists in September 2019, the Saudi state has issued 400,000 visas. The country now plans to do much more.

Still in this perspective of extending its influence and competing with its "media" neighbors, the Saudi state is looking to invest in a European club. Initial rumors suggested that Saudi Arabia wanted to buy Manchester United, which would have been a way to enter the world of soccer through the front door, since the English club is the third richest club in the world, with more

---

55. GOMEZ Carole, " Le sport, un levier d'influence pour l'Arabie Saoudite ", interview RFI, January 2020.

than 130 million fans worldwide, and has a turnover of more than 700 million euros for the year 2018/2019. A choice not insignificant, when we know that the other club of the English metropolis, Manchester City, belongs to Sheikh Mansour, member of the royal family of Abu Dhabi.

The piece is too big for the Saudi state, which sets its sights in 2019 on another English club, more affordable: Newcastle. For this takeover, the Saudis are partnering with Amanda Staveley, a British businesswoman already behind the purchase of Manchester City. Although the owner of the club is a seller and Saudi Arabia has a large nest egg with its sovereign wealth fund, estimated at more than $ 382 billion, the transaction will never happen. The reason is that the Saudi country hosts the pirate TV channel beOutQ, which, as its name suggests, hijacks the channels of the Qatari channels of the beIN Sports group. The Qatari media group is one of the main broadcasters of the Premier League, where Newcastle is present. At the political level, many voices across the UK have been raised against this Saudi investment, which is seen as *sportwashing* - the use of sport by an authoritarian state to cover up its actions. In the case of the Saudi regime, the finger was pointed at its numerous human rights violations. This set of challenges has prevented Saudi Arabia from realizing its plan to buy a major club in the world's most popular soccer league.

For Qatar, the goal remains to be the central country for sport in the 21st century. The Qatar Olympic Committee has set an ambitious goal of hosting 50 international competitions by 2030. It is already on its way with the setting up of the world handball championships in 2015, cycling in 2016, athletics in 2019 or swimming in 2023... And why not, later, the Olympic Games? This influence is not only to make the emirate shine, but also to diversify an

18. Qatar-Saudi Arabia: the new soccer duel?

economy dependent on the exploitation of fossil fuels. As for its Saudi neighbor.

The 2022 World Cup is shaping up to be *the* competition that could put Qatar in the big league. The national team, the 2019 Asian champions, composed mostly of national players, will be the main representative of the Qatari sports policy at this competition. That is why, until then, it is rushing to face the best teams in the world (participation in the Gold Cup, the Copa America or even, more surprisingly, in the qualifications of the European zone for their own World Cup!) so that the World Cup is a success both from the point of view of organization and in terms of results.

Paradoxically, this World Cup is discrediting the country more and more, due to the disastrous conditions in which the workers are working on the construction of the stadiums (6,500 workers are said to have died on these sites according to the newspaper *The Guardian*[56]), the energy and ecological costs of the event, numerous calls for a boycott... The queen of soccer competitions could finally tarnish the image of Qatar more than make this country shine in the eyes of the world, which is even being criticized by its Saudi neighbor under the pretext of *sportwashing.*

The very (too) offensive strategy of the Saudi state in this field does not deceive anyone for the moment, as witnessed for example by the recent women's golf tournament organized there, a historic moment for Saudi officials seeking to place themselves at the forefront of the development of women's sports; a moment strongly criticized by human rights associations, as women's freedoms in this kingdom are so reduced. The use of sport to radiate in the world has its limits. Petrodollars make it possible to organize, participate in, and be associated with the greatest sporting events.

---

56. MᴄIɴᴛʏʀᴇ Niamh, Pᴀᴛᴛɪssoɴ Pete, *op. cit.*

However, they cannot hide the poor human rights record of the Saudi regime.

In addition to the ecological question, Qatar must take this issue into account in the run-up to *its* World Cup if it does not want its sports empire to turn into a house of cards.

VI. Soccer,
an emancipation ground for the peoples

19.
1958-1962:
THE "ELEVEN OF INDEPENDENCE" OF ALGERIA

While the Algerian war was in full swing in 1958, the Algerian National Liberation Front (FLN) had the idea of creating a soccer team to mobilize French and international opinion on the country's independence. This team is much more than a simple selection. Through its prowess on and off the field, this "Eleven of Independence", with its uncomplicated and spectacular style of play, will travel the world in the name of a free Algeria.

"By your action, you have advanced the revolution by ten years."[57] This is how Ferhat Abbas, the first head of state of the Algerian Republic, expressed himself when he met the Algerian National Liberation Front (FLN) soccer team in 1961. A team composed mainly of professional players, which toured the world to promote the issue of Algerian independence internationally.

---

57. CORREIA Mickaël, *Une histoire populaire du soccer,* La découverte, 2018, p. 161.

After the Second World War, the Algerian territory was still under French control, and had been since 1830. However, the Algerian colony was declared by the Constitution of 1848 to be an integral part of France and divided into three departments (Algiers, Oran and Constantine). Over the years, the movement for Algerian independence grew and led to the creation of the Union populaire algérienne party in 1938 and the Manifeste du peuple algérien in 1943. The situation reached a point of no return on May 8, 1945, with the Sétif massacre, during which the French armed forces bloodily suppressed nationalist demonstrations. From that date on, the independence movement took on considerable importance.

Two events accelerated the process. First, the Arab revolution of 1952 in Egypt, which put an end to the British occupation. Second, the defeat of the French army at Diên Biên Phu in 1954, which brought the Indochina War to an end and symbolized the decline of the former French colonial empire. Following these events, France embarked on a process of decolonization, which led to the independence of Morocco and Tunisia in 1956. This is not the case of Algeria, because France considers this territory as an integral part of the metropolis - its subsoil, rich in fossil resources, especially in gas, is a significant strategic asset.

On November 1, 1954, the armed forces of the FLN launched nearly 70 attacks on French strategic points. This event, called the Red All Saints Day, was the starting point of the Algerian War of Independence. The conflict intensified from 1956 onwards, as nearly 450,000 French soldiers were mobilized in this war against 25,000 Algerian fighters, the *fellagas*. However, this conflict received little media coverage. The UN was slow to recognize Algeria's right to self-determination. France, for its part, described the situation as an internal police problem. In order to show that the conflict was almost non-existent, French Cup matches were organized on Algerian soil. However, it was thanks to football that the leaders of the FLN tried to find ways to expose their struggle for Algerian independence.

The idea emerged in 1956: to use the large contingent of professional Algerian players in metropolitan France (nearly thirty) to form a soccer team. Some of them already supported the cause by paying a revolutionary tax, which could represent up to 15% of their salary. The objective of this selection is to make the FLN team the standard-bearer of Algerian independence and an ambassador of the future country to build future international relations.

Mohamed Boumezrag, a former professional player and director of the Algerian regional subdivision of the French Football Federation (FFF), prepared the ground in 1957 by meeting several of the footballers likely to join such a project. On April 13, 1958, 9 Algerian footballers deserted their first division clubs. Among them, Mustapha Zitouni, a key player of the French team, but also players like Abdelaziz Ben Tifour, Mohamed Maouche or the young hopeful Rachid Mekhloufi, regularly called to the Blues. The shockwave is such that the next day, the newspaper *L'Équipe* headlines: "Nine Algerian footballers have disappeared.[58] A hard blow for the clubs, and especially for the French soccer team, which a month later must begin its preparation for the 1958 World Cup. A strong symbol too, since until now few public figures have been involved in the Algerian question. As Rachid Mekhloufi explains, "[few] French people knew what was happening in Algeria. The French people became aware when we left that there was an Algerian war, a war of liberation"[59].

---

58. *Ibid*, p. 156.
59. *Ibid*, p. 157.

All of the players met again in Tunisia on May 9, 1958. Barely a month after their flight, the National Liberation Front team played its first match against Morocco at the Chedly-Zouiten Stadium in Tunis. For the first time, the colors of independent Algeria are brandished in a stadium, the Algerian anthem is sung at the top of its lungs. This first match is also the first victory of this team, soon nicknamed the "Eleven of Independence". Two days later, *bis repetita*, it is the victory against Tunisia. The French reaction was not long in coming, as FIFA decided, under pressure from the FFF, to suspend the defectors and to sanction any federation or team that agreed to meet them officially. This has resulted in much more attention around this banned nomadic selection, which will include up to 32 players. As Mustapha Zitouni explains, "Our departure showed that the entire Algerian population was with the FLN, not just bandits and mercenaries. We were happy in France, we had situations, the population loved us. We were not against France, but against colonialism, against the people who were in Algeria and had monopolized the goods"[60].

In spite of the sanctions, the Algerian team played several clubs and national teams during its four years of existence, often under a different name. The Algerian team began its first international tour from May to July 1959 in Eastern Europe, since the USSR and the Soviet bloc looked favorably on any independent movement that could weaken the countries of the Western bloc. For the FLN, these international matches, between its team and that of "brotherly countries", should foreshadow the outline of future diplomatic relations of independent Algeria. Even if, on paper, the team plays against local teams, it is in fact the real national teams on the field. In every game, the Algerian team makes no attempt to hide and

---

60. *Ibid*, p. 158.

insists that these symbols be present. This leads to tensions with the Polish team, which agrees to play against the "Algerian Eleven" after the team threatened to boycott the match.

This European tour impresses. The footballers play in a liberated manner, in the image of the emancipation movement they want to defend. On the field, the FLN selection illustrates through its soccer the aspirations for collective emancipation of the Algerian people. A way of playing that pays off, with an average of 4 goals per game and a significant number of victories. In October 1959, the selection continues its media campaign and flies to Southeast Asia for a dozen games in China and North Vietnam. There, just after a match against a Vietnamese team, General Vo Nguyên Giap, winner of the battle of Diên Biên Phu, said to the Algerian players: "We beat the French, and you beat us in soccer. So you will beat France.[61]

This team reached its peak on March 29, 1961 in Belgrade, inflicting a real beating on the Yugoslavian team, finalist of the Euro 1960, with a victory by 6 goals to 1, under the eyes of the French ambassador present in the audience. The "Eleven of Independence" continued its journey until the signing of the Evian agreements between the French government and the provisional government of the Algerian Republic. These agreements put an end to the war and paved the way for Algeria's independence, officially proclaimed on July 5, 1962. As for soccer, suspensions were lifted and Algerian players could return to play for French clubs. After four years of touring the world, often in precarious conditions, the FLN team will have played nearly 91 games for 65 victories, 13 draws, 13 defeats, and played a key role in future Algerian diplomatic relations.

---

61. GHEMMOUR Chérif, *Terrain Miné, quand la politique s'immisce dans le soccer, op. cit*, p. 98.

20.

GREENLAND:

FOOTBALL AS A NEW PATH TO INDEPENDENCE

For some years now, Greenland, the world's largest island, has been plotting its course to become independent from Denmark. Although the Danish authorities are not totally against it, the climatic, diplomatic and economic obstacles to achieve it are numerous. Soccer, the country's most popular sport, could well be the icebreaker of these different obstacles towards greater autonomy.

"In Greenland, soccer connects everyone. We want to show that even though we are a small nation with so few people, we can play soccer at a high level."[62] Patrick Frederiksen, captain of one of Greenland's most important clubs, B-67, has a point. Football is quite simply the most popular sport in the country, with almost 10% of the population playing it. For some years now, soccer has been a great tool for emancipation in this large country on the Arctic border.

---

62. WARD Tom, "The inside story of Greenland's one-week soccer season," *Red Bull,* November 2019.

Greenland is indeed a huge island of more than 2 million km^2, but its geographical situation, located between the Arctic and Atlantic oceans, means that the territory is subject to strong climatic constraints, which force its 55,000 inhabitants to live on a narrow coastal strip. A "small" nation in a large territory, which is constantly attracting interest. Indeed, global warming is accelerating the melting of glaciers, which has increased four-fold between 2003 and 2013. Despite this ominous scenario, the opening of new trade routes offers opportunities to this too often forgotten territory.

It is true that, in the past, Greenland's position and climate have not really helped attract the curious. Although, according to legend, the name of the country, which means "green land", would have been given by Icelandic explorers to attract settlers to these hostile lands. It is only after the Second World War that the strategic position of the island begins to attract covetousness. Denmark was then occupied by Nazi Germany; Greenland could follow the same path, having been a Danish territory since 1814, which worried the United States, which feared an invasion. They therefore made the Arctic territory an advanced base. At the end of the war, the Americans offered to buy the island from Denmark for 100 million dollars. The offer was refused, although the American presence remained, with a large military base integrated into NATO since 1951, located in the town of Thule. As for Denmark, it opened Greenland to free trade and changed its status from a colony to a Danish province in 1953.

From this date on, the Danish government implemented a policy of cultural assimilation towards the Greenlanders. The more time passed, the more a movement developed in favour of greater autonomy for Greenland from the 1970s. Moreover, due to political complications related to Denmark's entry into the European Common Market in 1972, a reflection was carried out to seek a different status for Greenland. In 1979, Greenland was granted internal self-government status, with the creation of a parliament and a government with sovereignty over internal matters. In 1985, Greenland managed to leave the European Economic Community by referendum to protect its fishing zones, while Denmark remained in the Community. The differentiation is going to be accentuated since it is also at this period that Greenland adopts its own flag, red and white, which, according to its creator Thue Christiansen, represents the sun on the sea and the icebergs which drift on the waves, and takes back the Danish colors.

In 2009, this autonomy was reinforced following a referendum. Greenland is now co-sovereign in the management and exploitation of its subsoil resources, and Greenlandic becomes the official language. The country also has a constitutional right to self-determination, with the approval of Denmark. The path to independence seems to be taking shape: in 2016, the coalition government led by Prime Minister Kim Kielsen announced the creation of a ministry in charge of independence. The coalition agreement begins with the words, "Greenland is irrevocably on its way to independence."[63]

However, this road is far from being completely clear, as this territory is so economically dependent on Denmark. Despite its enormous mineral resources, the island's economy still relies exclusively on fishing and on economic aid from Denmark, to the tune of 500 million euros, which represents 60% of Greenland's budget. With its extreme temperatures, its enormous distances and its lack

---

63. SMITH Rory, "Soccer at the Edge of the World," *The New York Times*, September 2019.

of infrastructure, the exploitation of the subsoil, rich in hydro-carbons, is still extremely complex. Only two mines are currently in operation in the south of the island. These dotted economic perspectives do not push the Greenlanders to immediate indepen-dence, because they fear a drop in their standard of living.

Independence therefore requires economic autonomy, with major investments in infrastructure to exploit fossil resources and diversify the economy, inspired, for example, by the Icelandic model of developing local ecological tourism. The appetites of mining companies and states are numerous around Greenland and its subsoil. China and the United States, in particular, have their eye on the island's uranium deposits and strategic position.

To make its territory more attractive, soccer can be a lever to access independence and international recognition. Despite the climatic conditions, football is one of the most popular sports on the island, with nearly 5,000 members, i.e. almost 10% of the popu-lation, and nearly 70 clubs throughout the island. A championship has also been held since 1954, but the climate is such that it is played over a week. In 2019, to qualify for one of the 8 spots in the tournament, 40 teams from around the country participated in regional qualifiers. The development of soccer is supported by the Greenlandic political authorities to promote sports activities, and thus decrease the social problems related to alcoholism or suicides.

The soccer organization of the country is an old story: a Greenland Football Association was founded in 1971, a first stone to the construction of a national team. This team played its first international match on July 2, 1980 against the Faroe Islands, with a severe defeat (6 to 0). After several other matches against neighboring countries, Greenland began the process of becoming a member of FIFA in 1998, to participate in the World Cup qualifiers, a process that is far from being far-fetched since the world soccer organization accepts in its ranks countries that are not completely independent. This is the case, for example, of the Faroe Islands, also an autonomous territory of Denmark, which have been members of FIFA since 1988 and of UEFA since 1990.

To support its request, Greenland organizes international matches. The team made news on June 30, 2001, when it played against Tibet in Copenhagen. The match attracted international attention when China threatened to embargo Greenland's shrimp exports because of Tibet's disputed sovereignty. Despite Chinese pressure, the match will take place in Copenhagen's Vanløse Stadium. Nearly 5,000 supporters attended this historic meeting between two representatives of territories not recognized at the international level. The victory by 4 goals to 1 of Greenland on Tibet is anecdotal so much this match is carrying symbols for the two teams.

Since then, the large Arctic island has been trying to make a place for itself on the soccer planet. This goal is far from being achieved, since the Greenlandic association was refused membership in FIFA in 2010. Sepp Blatter said at the time: "According to the admission rules, for a soccer association to be admitted it must come from an independent state recognized by the international community, i.e. the UN, to apply for membership of FIFA."[64] The Faroe Islands case law could not be invoked because more restrictive membership rules were established in 2004. But since the handover of the FIFA presidency in 2015, the situation has changed, as Gibraltar, a British overseas territory claimed by Spain, or Kosovo, an internationally disputed state and non-member of the UN, are indeed members of UEFA and FIFA.

---

64. FIFA, "Greenland gripped by soccer fever", September 2010.

Another obstacle prevents Greenland from joining: infrastructure. Indeed, the "green island" cannot maintain a grassy field because of the permafrost that envelops the territory. To remedy this, Greenland authorities set up a partnership in 2015 with the Danish Football Federation to develop synthetic surfaces. Several fields have been installed in the country, including the national stadium in the capital Nuuk. An infrastructure that would be brought to move since the Greenlandic authorities are planning a new stadium, the Arktisk Stadion, which can accommodate more than 3,000 spectators.

With the help of Denmark, Greenland has a good chance of joining UEFA and FIFA if this development continues in the right direction. Or why not CONCACAF? the North and Central American Football Confederation, because of its proximity to the American continent. Greenland's handball and badminton federations have already turned to this option to give their athletes international stature and to compete with real national teams.

While waiting for Greenland to try to qualify for a soccer Euro, the "Polar Bears", the team's nickname, are preparing. The selection is indeed a member of CONIFA (see Chapter 12) and participates in the Football Island Games, sports games between the different Nordic islands, where the Greenlanders were finalists in the 2017 edition. In any case, the horizon seems to be brightening as this approach to emancipation through soccer is supported by Denmark and other Scandinavian countries. Allan Hansen, president of the Danish Football Association, said at the 2017 UEFA Congress: "Greenland is currently in the pre-accession phase. I am much more optimistic than I was five years ago."[65]

---

65. McGwin Kevin, "Greenland could soon be a step closer to joining the world of international soccer," *Arctic Now*, July 2017.

In any case, Greenland continues to attract international attention, and the next few years will be decisive for this country. The
recent discoveries of rare earth and uranium deposits will force
Greenlanders to choose between their economic sovereignty and
the defense of their environment, and thus to choose which path
they want to take to chart their way to independence.

21.

Easter Island:
Football to the rescue of the Rapa Nui

It was on April 6, 1722 that the Dutch navigator Jakob Roggeveen discovered a piece of land lost in the middle of the Pacific Ocean: Easter Island. The place is famous for its moai statues, but the population of this territory, the Rapa Nui, is gradually forgotten, exploited and forced into exile. To preserve their culture, the islanders have turned to soccer to escape their isolation.

Easter Island is a territory whose image is inseparable from that of the great statues that are the moai. However, behind the postcard, the indigenous population, the Rapa Nui, has been fighting for several years to have their rights respected. As activist Tuhiira Tucki Huke, a member of the Rapa Nui community, explains, "[i]t is difficult for a small people who are fighting all alone in the middle of the ocean for their rights, territory, possession of land, identity, culture, intangible and tangible heritage," in a statement that follows the broad media campaign in 2018 for the return of Rapa Nui cultural heritage.

These people have indeed been present for hundreds of years on this lost island in the Pacific Ocean. It was discovered by the navigator Jakob Roggeveen, who was searching for a new spice trade route for the Dutch West India Company. The explorer set foot on the island on April 6, 1722, Easter Day, and named his discovery Easter Island. During the 18th century, despite the passage of Spanish and British ships and the famous French explorer La Pérouse, the island territory was not subject to the covetousness of the colonizing powers. As British cartographer James Cook summarized in his logs, "No nation will ever fight for the honor of having explored Easter Island, there is no island in the sea which offers less refreshment and convenience for navigation than this."[66] The island is indeed a hostile and, above all, isolated land. The nearest inhabited territories are Pitcairn Island, 2,075 km away, and the Chilean coast, more than 3,500 km away.

This remoteness makes that the island is really inhabited only from the 13rd century. At the same time, for example, as the arrival of the first settlers on the Hawaiian Islands. The first to touch the soil of Easter Island were called the *Matamua*, the "first" in Maori; they founded the Rapa Nui culture. They gave the island the name Rapa Nui, which in the native language means "the navel of the world". The most famous aspect of this culture are the moai, these immense statues with human figures, sculpted in tuff. These mysterious effigies are often blamed for the collapse of the indigenous people. The construction of these giants would have, indeed, led to the drying up of the natural resources of the island, causing an "ecological suicide". The reality is much more complex. The clan wars and the construction of these statues should not obscure the Dantean

---

66. Cook James, *Logbook of voyages 1768-1779*, Erdmann, 2020.

environmental conditions of this territory, marked by earthquakes, droughts and tsunamis.

It is especially the arrival of invaders that is the cause of the eradication of the Rapa Nui population of the island. The numerous raids of slave traders from Peru made the local population go from 2,500 people at the beginning of the 18th century to only a hundred or so at the time of its annexation by Chile in 1888. For Emol Martín Lara, professor of history at the Catholic University Silva Henríquez, "[in] the nineteenth century, Peruvian ships came to get islanders and brought them back to the country to make slaves of them".[67] The passage under Chilean sovereignty constitutes a new era, which is not at all synonymous with hope for the rare Rapa Nui survivors. They were parked in the reserve of Hanga Roa, the largest city on the island, the rest being left to Chilean sheep breeders from the mainland.

It was not until 1966 that the locals finally received Chilean nationality and were allowed to leave the reserve. This relative freedom was short-lived as Chile fell into dictatorship after Pinochet's coup d'état in 1973. With the return to democracy in 1989, the rights of the Rapa Nui evolved and were definitively recognized, thanks to the 1993 law on the protection of indigenous peoples. The situation of Easter Island improved little by little, especially in terms of population. From 1,200 inhabitants in 1982, the island has grown to more than 7,500 today, about 60% of whom are of Rapa Nui origin. The development of infrastructures and the opening of Chile to the world have allowed the island to prosper, partly thanks to tourism.

These new prospects are prompting the indigenous people to demand greater autonomy. Easter Island is currently a province,

---

67. "RAPA NUI: why Easter Island is changing its name," *The Little Santiago Journal*, August 2018.

which also includes the uninhabited island of Sala y Gómez, located hundreds of kilometers to the east. This province has a "special regime" status, with powers similar to those of a regional government, but remains under the administration of the mainland region of Valparaíso. Such a situation has prompted the locals to demand more autonomy. Above all, they want their culture and heritage, too often scorned, to be considered and restored. As an example, only 14% of the island's land now belongs to the Rapa Nui, the rest to the Chilean state.

It is in this perspective that the local population is developing ways to promote its culture. Sport has its place. The island is particularly interested in rugby. In 2016, it organized the "Seven of Rapa Nui", a tournament that brought together rugby 7s teams from French Polynesia, Easter Island and mainland Chile. However, it is the game of football that offers the Rapa Nui people the opportunity to make their demands known to the world. Soccer is the most popular sport on the island. The very first Rapa Nui Football Federation was created in 1975, laying the foundations for a first team and then for the creation of a local championship composed of 12 teams. The island is unique in having a team representing a selection of its best players, the CF Rapa Nui, registered with the Chilean National Professional Football Association, which allows it to play, in theory, matches against other amateur and professional clubs in the country, within the framework of the federation's official competitions.

This "national team" made its first outing outside the island in 1996, with a match at the neighboring Juan Fernández archipelago. The result was a 5-3 win. The turning point came a decade later, on August 5, 2009, with the first professional soccer match on Easter Island: a Chilean Cup match against Colo Rao, one of the most popular clubs in the country. Roberto Araki Peña, a Rapa Nui player at the time, remembers: "We prepared for two months with Miguel Ángel Gamboa, who played in the 1982 World Cup in Spain with Chile. We lasted 30 minutes, but they beat us 4-0. FIFA called it the match of the century. That's exactly how it went down.[68] Despite the defeat, the interest of the match is, for Chile, to strengthen the links between the island and the continent, and to give it an international exposure with a broadcasting of the match in several countries - in Bolivia, Ecuador, Honduras and Argentina.

It is also an opportunity for the Rapa Nui to showcase their culture. Before the match, they perform a traditional warrior dance called *hoko*, similar to the *haka of* the New Zealand All Blacks in rugby. FIFA, which called this match the "match of the century", then helped the island to develop a soccer infrastructure. This was done with the construction of the 3,000-seat Rapa Nui Stadium in Hanga Roa, which was inaugurated in 2014 in the presence of Brazilian legend Pele and Chilean international player Elias Figueroa. The local mayor at the time, Pedro Edmunds, said of it, "We are proud that a personality like Pele came to such an important event for us. It gives visibility to a place like ours, which is one of the most isolated in the world, and an immense joy to all the inhabitants of the island.[69]

The Rapa Nui selection did not stop there, as it organized the *Campeonato nacional de fútbol de Pueblos Originarios* (National Championship of Indigenous Peoples) with seven other ethnic groups. It won the 2012 edition against the Mapuche team, an indigenous people from Chile and Argentina. The Easter Island team is

---

68. FIFA, "Football on Easter Island", April 2020.
69. DEPLANQUE Sébastien, "Rapa Nui, l'autre île du soccer," *La Grinta*, April 2019.

also looking to build ties with Polynesian selections, as evidenced by the Festival of Islands tournament. In their first participation in 2018, the Rapa Nui leave with a respectable record of two wins, one draw and two losses. The team's number 10, Tuki Muraccioli will say, "Some of us have been to Tahiti before, but this is the first time we've come as a team, as the Rapa Nui national soccer team in an official competition."[70] After this success, the players are returning for the 2019 edition with a larger delegation, including a women's soccer and futsal team.

Finally, the Rapa Nui team joined CONIFA in 2019, which could allow it to compete with other international teams, pending a possible membership in FIFA to participate in the World Cup qualifiers. However, such a membership seems compromised given the relative autonomy of the island and the poor soccer infrastructure.

However, things are moving in the right direction since in 2018, the indigenous people obtained from Chile the change of the name of Easter Island to Rapa Nui. The president of Chile, Sebastián Piñera, declared at the time, "We want to make an act of historical claim and recognize the thousand-year-old origin of the island." A speech far from being insignificant since, according to the activist Tuhiira Tucki Huke, if the Chilean authorities take the Rapa Nui claims in hand, it is to "show compassion for the Rapa Nui people, it makes Chile talk and it is beneficial for the image of the country, because Chile wants to position itself economically at the international level"[71]. This is a way of making people forget

---

70. Kucsera Kevin, "Festival of the Islands 2018: Rapa Nui joins the party!", Tahitian Football Federation, April 2018.
71. Bordron Maïwenn, Chaverou Éric, "Île de Pâques : le combat du peuple Rapa Nui pour la restitution de son patrimoine culturel", *France Culture*, November 2018.

the severe Chilean repression of the Rapa Nui demonstrations in the early 2010s.

Easter Island is nevertheless a fragile territory. The territory's economy is largely based on tourism. With approximately 100,000 tourists per year, the influx of visitors endangers the integrity of the island, already impacted by rising waters. This pushed the Chilean authorities to limit, in 2018, the tourist activity, now at a standstill with the Covid-19 pandemic. Sport and soccer will perhaps be the ultimate levers that will allow this isolated land to continue to exist.

22.
Tuvalu Islands:
SOCCER AS A WARNING ON GLOBAL WARMING

While the rise of the sea puts more than ever in danger the existence of island territories, the Tuvalu Islands, a small archipelago in the Pacific Ocean, decided to bet on soccer to alert on the global warming which threatens the very existence of their territory.

"No matter how much money you put on the table, that's not a valid reason not to do the right thing, which is to reduce your greenhouse gas emissions and not open new coal mines."[72] It was in these terms that Enele Sopoaga, former Prime Minister of Tuvalu, reacted to the 300 million dollars released by Australia, in September 2019, to help the Pacific islands. Territories that are on borrowed time due to the consequences of global warming.

The Tuvalu Islands are in this situation. Lost in the immensity of the Pacific Ocean, the 8 atolls of this archipelago (*Tuvalu* meaning "8 together" in the local language) have only 12,000 inhabitants.

---

72. ROY Ainge Eleanor, "'One day we'll disapear': Tuvalu's sinking islands," *The Guardian*, May 2019.

These lands have the particularity to be one of the narrowest territories in the world, the widest place being only 400 meters. These geographical constraints did not prevent the former British colony from becoming independent in 1978. It must be said that the creation of the United Nations, after the Second World War, led to a long process of decolonization, particularly with regard to the British colonies in the Pacific, to move towards self-determination.

This recent independence very quickly raised the question of economic sovereignty. With no natural resources of its own, the small archipelago had to turn to the sale of fishing licenses to emancipate itself and be recognized as a country in its own right. It joined the United Nations on 5 September 2000, becoming the 189th member of the organization. More surprisingly, this international recognition is also largely due to the Internet. One of the main sources of income for Tuvalu comes from the national top level domain name, the famous ".tv", which brings in millions of dollars per year. However, this unknown financial manna does not highlight the specificities of this island territory.

The territory is classified by the United Nations as a "least developed country" because of its limited economic development potential, lack of resources and vulnerability to external environmental events. This is why Tuvalu still relies heavily on an international sovereign wealth fund, funded by Australia and New Zealand. Tourism could be the solution to diversify the country's economy, but the poor infrastructure only allows about 2,000 visitors per year to reach them. However, the archipelago needs international visibility to survive. Rising waters threaten the integrity of the country, which could be the first country to be submerged within 50 years. The highest point of the islands is 4.6 meters above sea level and there is a great risk that they will disappear. And this, even if other studies, dating from 2018, have pointed to the fact that these islands, geologically dynamic, are increasing in size and would adapt to the evolution of sea level. This dotted future does not delay in any case the first consequences of climate change with an increase in cyclones, droughts and other natural disasters.

Relocation of the population to New Zealand and Australia is, for now, not being considered by Tuvaluan authorities. In 2015, Enele Sopoaga stated that "moving out of Tuvalu will not solve any climate change problem... If you move these people to the middle of industrialized countries, it will just increase their consumption and increase greenhouse gas emissions."[73]

In order to develop, to invest and to postpone the deadline, Tuvalu must reveal itself to the world. What better way than sport to fly the flag at a major media event?

It is done since 2007, because these islands of the Pacific are admitted within the International Olympic Committee (IOC). This allows them, in 2008, to participate in the most followed competition in the world, the Olympic Games. Since the Beijing edition, Tuvalu sends every four years to each Olympiad a small delegation, from one to three athletes. An international recognition through sport which takes all its place with its soccer team.

Football is one of the most popular sports in the country. One year after its independence, in 1979, its national team already participated in the South Pacific Games and faced Tahiti for its first match, on August 28, 1979. It ended in a severe defeat: 18-0! Three days later, the Tuvalu soccer team recorded its first international victory against Tonga.

---

73. Roy Ainge Eleanor, "'One day we'll disapear': Tuvalu's sinking islands," *The Guardian*, May 2019.

22. Tuvalu Islands: soccer as a warning on global warming

The international meetings are limited to this type of competition, since the archipelago is not part of the big FIFA family, despite repeated requests since 1987. It must be said that the world soccer organization has tightened the conditions for membership, especially in terms of sports infrastructure. It is this last point that Tuvalu lacks. Without membership, no participation in FIFA competitions, thus in the World Cup. Even if it is true that in case of membership, it would still be a long way to see Tuvalu in a World Cup. Since the departure of Australia from the Oceania confederation, New Zealand has been the great football nation of the continent, collecting tickets to the World Cup playoffs, as well as Oceania championships. Tuvalu have been investing since the early 2010s to improve. Unfortunately, the team cannot play at home, as the Tuvalu Sports Ground is located on a clay and dented ground. A solution has been found with their neighbors, Fiji, who are offering their stadium and training center to the Tuvalu Federation - a temporary solution that is far from sufficient in the eyes of FIFA.

This does not prevent the team to face the other Pacific countries. Tuvalu even participated in the qualifying rounds of the 2010 World Cup! This situation was made possible because the 2007 South Pacific Games were then considered as the first stage of qualification for the World Cup[74]. We can even say that Tuvalu got their first point in a World Cup qualification match, since they drew against Tahiti during these games. Viliamu Sekifu became the first Tuvaluan scorer in the history of the World Cup.

Although the islanders lost most of their games, the interest was elsewhere: playing an international competition and promoting their flag. The federation's limited financial resources and

---

74. FREW Craig, "Tuvallu still dreams of joingin FIFA's world soccer family," *BBC Sport*, December 2013.

high travel costs forced the team to become less active in the late 2000s. It only came back thanks to partnerships with other countries. This is the case since 2009, with the Dutch Support project, which forges close links between the Netherlands and Tuvalu, and results in the recruitment, in 2011, of a new Dutch coach, Foppe de Haan, currently the youth coach of Heerenveen. In 2013, Tuvalu also participated in a three-month tour of the Netherlands to play local teams.

At the international level, Tuvalu competes against other teams than their Oceanian neighbors, such as the United Koreans of Japan, Tamil Eelam or the Chagos Islands. This is made possible by the fact that the archipelago joined CONIFA in 2016. The Tuvalu participate in the 2018 CONIFA World Cup in London, with unfortunately three defeats against Matabeleland, Padania and Sicily. Sport remains today the best asset of Tuvaluans to make known the situation of their small nation and thus alert on the issue of climate refugees and save what can still be of the biodiversity of our planet. As Enele Sopoaga said during the COP21 in Paris in 2015, "Let's do it for Tuvalu, because if we save Tuvalu, we save the world."[75]

And what if soccer could be that whistleblower that will change the fate of the world?

---

75. Roy Ainge Eleanor, "'One day we'll disapear': Tuvalu's sinking islands," *The Guardian*, May 2019.

Acknowledgements

I would like to thank my brother Anthony in particular for having passed on to me this passion for soccer and geography since my childhood.

Thanks to my other half, Zoé, who supported and motivated me throughout this project with her advice, her precious feedback and especially her love.

Thanks to my mother, Nadège, unfailing support, whatever my projects and the obstacles to overcome.

Thank you to Jean-Charles Gérard, my editor, and Pascal Boniface for helping me with this book project.

Thanks to my family and all my relatives. In particular to the "club" of reviewers Florian, François, Geoffrey, Guillaume M., Guillaume C., Mathieu, Myriem, Romain and Sarah.

Thank you to all the subscribers of the Football Club Geopolitics for feeding this project with your interest and support.

Finally, a thought for my grandmother, Pierrette, who, I know, will read these lines with emotion.

In homage to my grandfather Aurelio, who was the first to tell me beautiful stories.

BIBLIOGRAPHY AND SOURCES

General works

ARCHAMBAULT Fabien, BEAUD Stéphane, GASPARINI William, *Le Football des nations :des terrains de jeu aux communautés imaginées,* Éditions de la Sorbonne, 2018.

BONIFACE Pascal, *Geopolitics of Sport*, Armand Colin, 2014.

BONIFACE Pascal, *JO politiques*, Eyrolles, 2016.

BONIFACE Pascal, *L'Empire foot : comment le ballon rond a conquis le monde*, Armand Colin, 2018.

CORREIA Mickaël, *A popular history of soccer,* La découverte, 2018.

DIETSCHY Paul, *History of soccer,* Perrin, 2010.

GHEMMOUR Chérif, *Terrain Miné, quand la politique s'immisce dans le soccer*, Hugo Sport, 2013.

GUÉGAN Jean-Baptiste, *Géopolitique du sport, une autre explication du monde*, Bréal, 2017.

WAHL Alfred, *La Balle au pied. History of soccer,* Gallimard, 1990.

Chapter 1

BARCELO Laurent, "L'Europe des 52". L'Union Européenne de Football Association (UEFA)", *Guerres mondiales et conflits contemporains* n° 228, October 2007.

GASPARINI William, *L'Europe du soccer, socio-histoire d'une construction européenne,* Presses universitaires de Strasbourg, 2017.

GERMAIN Guillaume, *1960-2020: 60 years of Euro soccer,* Jérôme Do Bentzinger editor, 2020.

MOUTON Olivier, *Hors-Jeu. 22 soccer matches that made history,* Armand Colin, 2017.

Chapter 2

GERMAIN Guillaume, *1960-2020: 60 years of Euro soccer,* Jérôme Do Bentzinger editor, 2020.

MOUTON Olivier, *Hors-Jeu. 22 soccer matches that made history,* Armand Colin, 2017.

- Internet sources

GOUBIN Thomas, "1964: Spain pays the USSR," *So Foot,* May 2012.

LUKOVIC Viktor, "A Euro 1960 between Soviets and Francoists", *Footballski,* April 2018.

Chapter 3

GERMAIN Guillaume, *1960-2020: 60 years of Euro soccer,* Jérôme Do Bentzinger editor, 2020.

MOUTON Olivier, *Hors-Jeu. 22 soccer matches that made history,* Armand Colin, 2017.

TRÉGOURÈS Loïc, *Football in the Yugoslav chaos,* Non Lieu, 2019.

- Internet sources

CHOWDHURY Saj, "Euro 1992: Denmark's fairytale," BBC Sport, May 2012.

GHEMMOUR Chérif, PEDRO Alexandre, "Once upon a time Richard-Moller Niesen and Denmark 1992," *So Foot*, February 2014.

Chapter 4

COLOVIC Ivan, *Politics of Identity in Serbia*, NYU Press, 2002.

RIVA Gigi, *The Last Penalty*, Seuil, 2016.

TRÉGOURÈS Loïc, *Football in the Yugoslav chaos*, Non Lieu, 2019.

WILSON Jonathan, *Behind the Curtain. Travels In Eastern European Football*, Orion Publishing Co, 2006.

- Internet sources

GHEMMOUR Chérif, "Le jour où Boban a réalisé son high kick", *So Foot*, May 2020

Chapter 5

PERRYMAN Marc, *Ingerland: Travels With a Football Nation*, Simon & Schuster, 2006.

- Internet sources

GIBBONS Michael, "The cultural resonance of Euro 96," *The Guardian*, July 2016.

NAKRANI Sachin, "Golden goal: Paul Gascoigne for England *v.* Scotland (1996)," *The Guardian*, December 2014.

WILSON Richard, "20 years of regret from Euro 96 loss," *BBC Sport*, June 2016.

Chapter 6

- Internet sources

Boffey Daniel, "Mind our language: Bulgaria blocks North Macedonia's EU path," *The Guardian*, November 2020.

Perrier Fabien, "Greece recognizes the name 'North Macedonia,'" *Le Temps*, January 2019.

Editor, "Football: a united North Macedonia celebrates its qualification for the Euro", *The Balkan Courier*, November 2020.

Chapter 7

Irak Dağhan, *Football Fandom Protest and Democracy. Supporter activism in Turkey*, Routledge, 2019.

- Internet sources

Cultures Monde (Florian Delorme's program), "Le sport, arme de séduction massive (2/4). Turkish soccer; a tool of nationalism, ferment of contestation", *France Culture*, January 2020.

Houeix Romain, "Football: the Başakşehir, a Turkish champion who owes a lot to Erdoğan," *France 24*, July 2020.

Katalenic Antun, "On the Football Pitch, Orban woos Hungarians abroad," *Balkan Insight*, January 2019.

Chapter 8

Archambault Fabien, Beaud Stéphane, Gasparini William, *The Football of Nations: from playing fields to imagined communities*, Éditions de la Sorbonne, 2018.

- Internet sources

Boy Louis, "Four years after the annexation by Russia, the slow decline of soccer in Crimea," *Franceinfo*, June 2018.

CANDAU Adrien, "Crimea, the bullet in the foot," *So Foot*, June 2018.

MOSKO Alexei, "Crimea wants to become a full-fledged soccer nation," *Russia Beyond*, November 2016.

Chapter 9

TRÉGOURÈS Loïc, *Football in the Yugoslav chaos*, Non Lieu, 2019.

LEFEVRE Florian, "Fadil Vokrri", *So Foot*, June 2020.

- Internet sources

AMES Nick, "Kosovo's dream team is ready to inspire a more hopeful future," *The Guardian*, September 2019.

Chapter 10

- Internet sources

McELWEE Molly, "The inside story of how Gibraltar has stunned soccer," *The Telegraph*, November 2018.

MONTAGUE James, "Gibraltar moves closer to soccer independence," *New York Times*, May 2013.

PENALBA SOTORRIO Mercedes, "Gibraltar: a history of ill will over the Rock," *The Conversation*, April 2017.

Chapter 11

- Internet sources

AFP, "Europa League: in Baku, sport as a showcase for the regime," May 2019.

COLLIN Jean-Christophe, "De retour du front, les footballeurs du Haut-Karabakh retrouvent le terrain", *L'Équipe*, December 2020.

DOYLE Paul, "Why did UEFA hand Azerbaijan hosting rights for the Europa League final?", *The Guardian*, May 2019.

Chapter 12

- Internet sources

Duez Julien, "We were at the CONIFA World Cup final," *So Foot*, June 2018.

Menetier Denis, "Comté de Nice, Ruthénie subcarpatique, Abkhazie... bienvenue à la CONIFA, l'antichambre de la FIFA", *France TV Sport*, February 2021.

Weeks Jonny, "The Alternative World Cup," *The Guardian*, June 2018.

Chapter 13

- Internet sources

Dowling Tim, "The World Cup sides you've never heard of", *The Guardian*, June 2008.

Kejonen Olle, "1985: Sápmis första landskamp," *Sverige Radio*, August 2015.

Pave Linn Margrete, "Nytt Samisk fotballforbund - FA Sápmi," *NRK Sápmi*, May 2014.

Chapter 14

- Internet sources

Chadband Ian, "San Marino hero who humiliated England," *Evening Standard*, March 2003.

Hughes Rebecca Ann, "A Historic Season for the world's worst national soccer team," *Forbes*, December 2020.

Pauluzzi Valentin, interview with Andy Sellva, *So Foot*, March 2015.

Chapter 15

GHEMMOUR Chérif, *Terrain Miné, quand la politique s'immisce dans le soccer*, Hugo Sport, 2013.

Kapuściński Ryszard, *The Soccer War,* Granta Books, 1990.

- Internet sources

CALMARD Diego, "50 years ago, the Honduras-Salvador match triggered the 'soccer war,'" *Mediapar* "blogs," June 2019.

Chapter 16

- Internet sources

AUBRY Émilie, "Hong Kong: the end of freedom? Une leçon de géopolitique", *Arte* ("Le dessous des cartes"), December 2020.

DE CHANGY Florence, "À Hongkong, la loi de sécurité imposée par la Chine met brutalement à fin à une exception démocratique", *Le Monde,* July 2020.

Ross Donald, "China National Team. The 5.19 incident: China's doomed attempt to qualify for Mexico 86," *WideEastFootball.net,* October 2017.

WOOD Chris, "When Hong Kong beat China in a World Cup qualifier 32 years ago, and riots that followed," *South China Morning Post,* May 2017.

Chapter 17

GHEMMOUR Chérif, *Terrain Miné, quand la politique s'immisce dans le soccer*, Hugo Sport, 2013.

- Internet sources

BRIGAND Maxime, "Argentina-England 1986, the whim of God", *So Foot,* November 2020.

Carlin John, "England vs Argentina - A history", *The Guardian*, May 2002.

Cavalonne Elena, "With Brexit, uncertainty looms over the future of the Falkland Islands," *Euronews,* January 2021.

Garric Audrey, "Les Malouines, trente ans de conflit irrésolu," *Le Monde*, April 2012.

Chapter 18

Blake Heidi and Calvert Jonathan, *The Ugly Game: The Qatari Plot to Buy the World Cup,* Simon&Chuster, 2016.

Guégan Jean-Baptiste, *Géopolitique du sport, une autre explication du monde*, Bréal, 2017.

- Internet sources

Chadwick Simon, "Why Saudi Arabia won't buy an English soccer team," *Policy Forum,* February 2020.

Conn David, "Qatar 2022: £40 a week to build the World Cup stadiums," *The Guardian*, November 2018.

Gomez Carole, "Le sport, un levier d'influence pour l'Arabie saoudite," RFI interview, January 2020.

Le Magoariec Raphaël, "Qatar's strategy to become a soccer great," *Orient XXI*, November 2016.

McIntyre Niamh, Pattisson Pete, "Revealed: 6,500 migrant workers have died in Qatar since World Cup awarded," *The Guardian*, February 2021.

Zidan Karim, "Sportswashing: how Sauda Arabia lobbies the US's largest sports bodies," *The Guardian*, September 2019.

Chapter 19

Correia Mickaël, *A popular history of soccer,* La découverte, 2018.

Ghemmour Chérif, *Terrain Miné, quand la politique s'immisce dans le soccer*, Hugo Sport, 2013.

- Internet sources

Rouaba Ahmed, "The incredible story of Algeria's 'independence dribblers,'" *BBC Africa*, May 2018.

Chapter 20

- Internet sources

Knox Tomos, "The unlikely success stroye of soccer on the massive island of Greenland," *These Football Times*, October 2014.

McGwin Kevin, "Greenland could soon be a step closer to joining the world of international soccer," *Arctic Now*, July 2017.

Petite Simon, "Greenland and the Faroe Islands: in the North, independence in small steps," *Le Temps*, April 2018.

Editor, "Football in Greenland," *Nordisk Football*, October 2017.

Smith Rory, "Soccer at the Edge of the World," *The New York Times*, September 2019.

Ward Tom, "The inside story of Greenland's one-week soccer season," *Red Bull*, November 2019.

Chapter 21

- Internet sources

Bordron Maïwenn, Chaverou Éric, "Île de Pâques : le combat du peuple Rapa Nui pour la restitution de son patrimoine culturel", *France Culture*, November 2018.

Deplanque Sébastien, "Rapa Nui, l'autre île du soccer," *La Grinta*, April 2019.

FIFA, "Football on Easter Island", April 2020.

Kucsera Kevin, "Festival of the Islands 2018: Rapa Nui joins the party!", Tahitian Football Federation, April 2018.

Long Gilden, "Easter Island has soccer debut," *BBC News*, August 2009.

"RAPA NUI: why Easter Island is changing its name," *The Little Santiago Journal*, August 2018.

Chapter 22

- Internet sources

Bisogno Dominic José, "What Tuvalu and Kiribati's growing inclusion could mean for both nations and the OFC," *These Football Times*, June 2020.

Frew Craig, "Tuvallu still dreams of joingin FIFA's world soccer family," *BBC Sport*, December 2013.

Roy Ainge Eleanor, "'One day we'll disapear': Tuvalu's sinking islands," *The Guardian*, May 2019.

Table of Contents

Best sellers Max Milo Editions

Hitler's banker, Jean-François Bouchard

Confessions of a forger, Éric Piedoie Le Tiec

The Koran and the flesh, Ludovic-Mohamed Zahed

Governing by fake news, Jacques Baud

Governing by chaos, Collectif

A political history of food, Paul Ariès

Mad in U.S.A.: The ravages of the "American model",
Michel Desmurget

Mondial soccer club geopolitics, Kévin Veyssière

Putin: Game master?, Jacques Braud

Treatise on the three impostors: Moses, Jesus, Muhammad,
The Spirit of Spinoza

TV Lobotomy, Michel Desmurget